HOW TO ENSURE ED/TECH IS NOT OVERSOLD AND UNDERUSED

HOW TO ENSURE ED/TECH IS NOT OVERSOLD AND UNDERUSED

**Edited by
Arthur D. Sheekey**

Foreword by
Larry Cuban

Afterword by
Laurence Peters

A SCARECROWEDUCATION BOOK

The Scarecrow Press, Inc.
Lanham, Maryland, and Oxford
2003

A SCARECROWEDUCATION BOOK

Published in the United States of America
by Scarecrow Press, Inc.
A Member of the Rowman & Littlefield Publishing Group
4501 Forbes Boulevard, Suite 200, Lanham, Maryland 20706
www.scarecroweducation.com

PO Box 317
Oxford
OX2 9RU, UK

British Library Cataloguing in Publication Information Available

Library of Congress Cataloging-in-Publication Data
How to ensure ed/tech is not oversold and underused / [edited by] Arthur D.
Sheekey.
    p. cm.
"A ScarecrowEducation book."
Includes bibliographical references and index.
  ISBN 0-8108-4620-9 (pbk. : alk. paper)
  1. Educational technology—United States. 2. Computer-assisted
instruction—United States. 3. Teachers—In-service training—United States.
I. Sheekey, Arthur D.
LB1028.3 .H672 2003
371.33—dc21   2002013871

♾™ The paper used in this publication meets the minimum requirements of
American National Standard for Information Sciences—Permanence of
Paper for Printed Library Materials, ANSI/NISO Z39.48-1992.
Manufactured in the United States of America.

CONTENTS

ACKNOWLEDGMENTS

The grant for the support of the Appalachian Technology in Education Consortium Project, located at The CNA Corporation, provided the funds to commission the papers that evolved into the nine chapters in this book. The grant (R 302 A000014) originated from the Office of Educational Research and Improvement (OERI) in the U.S. Department of Education. In addition to recognizing OERI and the work of its dedicated program managers, I thank my colleagues in the Institute for Public Research at The CNA Corporation. I am grateful to Larry Cuban, a colleague and friend, whose talks and writing have stimulated the recent public policy debate about the impact educational technology is having on improving and reforming schools. I would also like to express my appreciation to Tom Koerner, editorial director for ScarecrowEducation Books, a Division of Scarecrow Press, Inc., who encouraged me to undertake this publication and whose periodic inquiries about the status of the manuscript were an important catalyst for completing the manuscript that we promised to deliver.

FOREWORD

Larry Cuban
Stanford University

Education policymakers must give serious consideration to all the key factors that shape what teachers do everyday in their classrooms once they close their doors.

Over the past year, I have been meeting with teachers, administrators, national and state policymakers, and district board members across the nation, all of whom were eager to talk about their experiences using computers for instruction. Many had read *Oversold and Underused*; others had heard about the book and the research that I had reported. Many wanted me to answer their questions, tell me where I had erred, and raise issues of deep concern to them that I had neglected to cover in the book. In reading the foregoing accounts from teachers, technology coordinators, and administrators who wrote of their experiences with new technologies, I thought of those many exchanges I have had. This publication gives me the chance to offer three observations on what I have learned from these largely positive, even glowing, written accounts and those intense discussions.

   1. Conversations about computers in schools have become less testy, less polarizing, and more engaging in their policy implications.

2. The notion that the computer is a learning tool is firmly planted in the language used to describe new technologies, yet integrating the tool into the daily repertoire of teachers remains the ultimate challenge.

3. In the minds of both practitioners and policymakers, the individual teacher remains the dominant and sole reason why new technologies fail to be used frequently and imaginatively for classroom instruction. Organizational and political structures within and without the school continue to be ignored as substantial factors that help shape daily teaching.

Let me briefly elaborate on each of these observations.

1. *Conversations about computers in schools have become less testy, less polarizing, and more engaging in their policy implications.* Name calling, at least public scorn for anyone who would question the prevailing belief in the magical efficacy of computers in schools, is unfashionable. I found educators and noneducators who deeply believed in classroom computers as engines of learning and were willing to listen to one another and critics when concerns were raised about the unreliability of the technologies, the lack of adequate software, and insufficient technical support.

In the past, promoters of new technologies, whether they were practitioners or policymakers, would curtly dismiss these concerns by calling the persons "Luddites." No more, at least in public. As investments in new technologies continue to mount, as the all-important algorithm of total-cost-of-operations has sunk into the skulls of policymakers, and as recession-driven fiscal retrenchment has reduced school budgets, there is far more willingness on the part of ardent promoters to pause and consider answers to tough questions: Do teachers integrate the new technologies into their daily instruction? If not, why not? How much of the technology budget is spent on on-site professional development of teachers? Is on-site technical support available to teachers? What software is available that is aligned to the district's curricular standards? Has academic achievement (or critical thinking, or civic engagement) improved as a consequence of teacher use of classroom technologies? That these questions could be asked and thoughtfully considered is encouraging. I hope this trend will continue sufficiently for skeptics and advocates to be able to learn from one another and act together.

2. *The notion that the computer is a learning tool is firmly planted in the language used to describe new technologies, yet integrating the tool into the daily repertoire of teachers remains the ultimate challenge.* Time and again, the refrain that the computer (and its software) is no more than a learning tool, a means to a larger educational end, came from school board members and teachers, superintendents, and parents. And based on the testimony of those who have written about their experiences, the clever and imaginative ways that the new technologies can be used routinely in teaching and learning are more than evident. No more did I hear (or read) that somehow, in some way, these miracle-machines would revolutionize the classroom. I consider the shift in vocabulary, the downsizing of expectations about the technology to fit the vocabulary of classroom tools and teaching repertoires, to be a small victory for common sense about schooling in America.

But a victory in talk is a far cry from concrete action, particularly for teachers to make it part of their daily classroom routines. Integration (or "infusion" as some advocates labeled it) of the new technologies into classroom teaching remains confined to a tiny minority of practitioners. Most practitioners still see the software and hardware as "add-ons" to the daily chores expected of them and what they expect of themselves. As a consequence, serious and occasional users have their students do word processing, Internet searches, and similar low-level tasks on machines loaded with powerful interactive software. Such use has been characterized by promoters of integrated use of these tools as unimaginative—the least offensive term that I have heard. Whether it is the lack of adequate software, sufficient on-site help from teacher coaches, technical support for equipment breakdowns, or some combination of these and other factors, the optimal conditions for integration remain far out of the reach of most practitioners.

Fortunately, the customary teacher bashing that has accompanied early efforts to introduce technological innovations in classrooms is largely absent. What has replaced finger pointing is the much softer form of indirect censure that is suggested by the often-stated solution of more and better training of preservice and in-service teachers to use technology. This all-purpose strategy of getting teachers to use the new technologies regularly and creatively as part of their daily repertoire and not as an add-on avoids criticizing teachers directly but again construes the problem of integration of computers as an individual problem that can be solved by more education. Which brings me to my third observation.

3. *In the minds of both practitioners and policymakers, the individual teacher remains the dominant and sole reason why new technologies fail to be used frequently and imaginatively for classroom instruction. Organizational and political structures within and without the school continue to be ignored as substantial factors that help shape daily teaching.* In these readings and in all of the discussions I have participated in, I have been struck again and again by how highly informed and well-regarded promoters of new technologies in schools framed both the problem and solution. The problem of infrequent and uncreative classroom use was the teacher; the solution was more skill training. Occasionally, eager advocates would point to the school as a workplace and consider the substantial differences in use between elementary and secondary teachers, but not for long. That organizational conditions built into the very DNA of the age-graded school for the past century and a half might have something to do with how teachers teach, the content that teachers cover, the social organization of the classroom, and how teachers assess student performance seldom held the attention of technology advocates for very long. Few of the readings dally on the organizational conditions that make the school and classroom a complex and demanding workplace.

Nor did most of my discussions and these readings consider seriously the political context of schooling such as the many expectations of policymakers and parents for what schools must do and the socioeconomic inequalities that have made urban public schools even more segregated by class and race than they were a quarter-century ago. Nor did we seriously consider the computer as a political symbol of modernity and the inexorable demands of employers, parents, and policymakers that the machines be both available and visible in schools. These political conditions have powerful effects on both teachers and students using computers as a tool for learning.

I raise these organizational and political factors because the policymaking debate over using computers in schools is dominated by an individualistic framing of the problem and solution rather than a serious consideration of all the key factors that shape what teachers do everyday in their classrooms once they close their doors.

In these observations, I have noted some progress in the way that critics and promoters are beginning to listen to one another and the language they use. I have also noted that the framing of the problem of teacher use continues to be narrowly focused on improving individual teachers without much consideration of the school as an organization and political institution. I believe that when all of these factors are analyzed and considered, issues of infrequent, limited, and nonintegrated use of technologies in schools can be seen in their entirety, and that more comprehensive strategies to use computers as teaching and learning tools will become candidates for action.

INTRODUCTION

Arthur D. Sheekey

The CNA Corporation

Soon after Harvard University Press released copies of Larry Cuban's latest book, *Oversold and Underused: Computers in the Classroom, Washington Post* journalist Jay Mathews wrote: "So what happened? We have wired up. We have gone online. We have partnered ourselves to Apple, Microsoft, Gateway, and Pepsi-Cola. We have created and crossed over the digital divide. We are somewhere past dawn. Yet the fundamental problems remain. Why?"[1] Mathews and many others who reviewed or commented on Larry Cuban's book suggested that his research provided some of the answers. Although Cuban's book provides insights into the difficulties of integrating computers and Web-based services in schools and classrooms, many of our colleagues in the field responded in a different and less complimentary way. During several national and state conferences and workshops with educators, we often heard comments such as, "Larry Cuban's analysis is shortsighted," "Larry Cuban apparently visited too few or the wrong schools," or "This is just another example of a university professor who wants to publish books." Larry Cuban's argument has clearly struck a nerve—one that has caught the attention of policymakers and the general public, which does not like to hear about misspending on education.

Over the past year, Larry Cuban has participated in dozens of conferences attended by educational researchers and practitioners. As Cuban
indicates in the foreword, he listened to his critics and held his ground.
Those who may have questioned Cuban's research methodology or
knowledge about the day-to-day operation of schools immediately recognized his appreciation and understanding of how classrooms and
teachers operate. Unlike many of the advocates and critics of educational technology, Cuban has had a long academic career that has involved teaching history in an inner city school, writing texts on U.S. history, and serving as an urban school superintendent. In short, he is well
prepared to defend his research findings and to interpret data derived
from research in ways that many other researchers cannot.

The idea for this book came about after listening to Cuban explain
what he found in schools and classrooms while at the same time hearing
from friends and colleagues who kept saying, "I wish Larry Cuban had
gone to this school or that school, or visited [some particular teacher]'s
classroom." We were told about the efforts of individual teachers and
educational technology coordinators who are making effective and productive use of computers and the Internet to achieve higher academic
standards for all their students. We set out to locate the good stories and
the individuals who could write about them. No scientific or systematic
approach was used to identify the authors whose papers are included in
this book. We merely asked a number of colleagues and state educational technology directors: "Have you come across an individual who
was effectively using and integrating educational technology in schools
and classrooms?"[2] After talking and communicating with a number of
these potential "stars" and learning of their readiness to write down
their own stories, we asked the candidates to participate in this project.
We asked them to complete a paper describing what they were doing
and what they were learning about the best ways to use educational
technology.

Not all of the authors stuck to the original outline, but they provided
the corroborating evidence that explains why their work was brought to
our attention. In addition to asking the authors to describe the situations
and conditions that contributed to effective use of educational technology, we asked them to "refer directly or indirectly to recent research
findings and claims, such as those included in Larry Cuban's book,

Oversold and Underused: Computers in the Classroom." Each received
a copy of the book, but apparently some did not feel compelled to suggest the relevance of their experience to the findings and recommendations in Cuban's book. Surprisingly, several of our writers, who were
identified as "experts" and "advocates for educational technology," did
not totally disagree with Larry Cuban's research findings.

The eleven authors were asked to describe the condition of their
schools or school systems (who is being served, etc.) and what each is attempting to accomplish, such as achieving state or local educational
standards. We also asked, "What do you see as the benefits of technology or telecommunications services in helping students learn and become engaged in educational activities?" They were urged to identify
the favorable and unfavorable conditions that influence the effective use
of technology, and, if they were up to it, the extent to which they agreed
or disagreed with "those who may be overly optimistic or overly pes-
simistic about the prospects of technology." We also suggested they address the question: "Are technology and telecommunications services
beginning to transform the nature of teaching and learning, and how
might they transform the delivery of education?"

In addition to answering these questions, we asked the writers to
identify the resources involved, including the types of technologies and
online services being used and how they are changing the way teachers,
students, and their families are benefiting: "Based on your personal observations and professional experience, we would like you to explain
how the operation of your school, school system, or program is different
and how the technologies and/or online services are making a difference." We also asked that they cite the critical challenges, such as what
they needed to overcome or change, or what needs to be in place to use
the technology effectively. Finally, we indicated that they could refer to
studies and findings, such as Cuban's, and include suggestions for what
needs to be done and by whom to ensure that investments in learning
technologies and electronic networks transform, improve, or extend
pre-K–12 education.

The eleven educational practitioners who responded to the set of
challenging questions we presented describe their involvement in local
or statewide initiatives that are designed to improve teaching and learning with the help of a wide array of learning technologies. They are all

committed to improving public education. They all truly believe that the systematic application of these technologies can transform the operations of elementary and secondary schools. Several of the authors admit that promoters and policymakers have oversold educational technologies and that computers in their own schools are underused. The government has poured roughly $50 billion into educational technology programs and, as a result, a huge amount of technology has been pushed into the operation of many ill-prepared school buildings. Fortunately, and as the content of this publication confirms, lessons have been learned. Each of our authors identifies several of the conditions required to successfully implement educational technology programs and services. Education policymakers, particularly state and local officials, would benefit from the experiences and approaches that are explained by the authors.

The conditions that are needed to successfully introduce and sustain educational programs and services that make use of advanced technologies are similar to those that are needed to support any new educational initiative. The educational technology programs that our authors describe involve decisions in choosing new and experimental approaches. These decisions determine how teachers are to be trained; what educational technologies and software will be purchased and used; and how state, school district, or school building officials will measure the success of the projects. All of these successful projects involve cooperative arrangements and partnerships, and those in lower income areas require federal funding.

The editors and sponsors of this volume have benefited from the lessons being learned from each of the projects. It is our intention to share these model programs with education policymakers who are in positions to influence state and local policies and investment strategies for educational technology. Within every region of the country, there are projects and initiatives that are similar to those we have recognized. The successful implementation and integration of technology in schools will require changes in the way teachers are trained. The projects being carried out by Robert Tai and his colleagues at the University of Virginia recognize that preservice and in-service teachers need to spend more time developing teaching strategies that relate to their own schools' curricular and student needs. The local school projects described by James

Eschenmann and Christine Richards demonstrate the impact of state standards and the new collaborative relationship that must be developed between state and local officials.

The projects described by Blake West, Tom Pfundstein, and Diane Reed reflect local leadership and sophistication on the part of individuals who are entrepreneurial and risk takers. However, they are operating in schools and districts that have created the conditions for their success. We suggest that such sites should be recognized as testbeds, that is, sites that should be visited by teams of policymakers and officials who want to witness what can work under the best circumstances. Finally, we present two projects in the state of Tennessee that reflect enlightened state leadership and an impressive degree of professionalism at the local level. The successful projects described by Diane Bennett, Mary Haney, and Elaine Wilkins attest to the advantages of federal grants that, in these cases, enabled teams of teachers to identify the critical needs of their students, exploit the full potential of available technologies, and demonstrate results that respond to state standards and the satisfaction of parent and local community groups.

Finally, we want to remind readers that in addition to the projects described in this publication, there are many others that deserve to be recognized. Some of the projects and experiences we are sharing have benefited from federal grants, which we estimate provided nearly $4 billion in 2001 for educational technology to states and local school districts. In fact, the conditions for success that are cited by the authors in this volume, as well as by so many others in the field, would not have come about without access to the discretionary funds that were authorized under the Technology Innovation Challenge Grant (TICG) program. All of the projects supported by the TICG program are listed and described on the U.S. Department of Education's website, www.ed.gov/Technology/challenge.

We have little hard data to document the effect of educational technology on student achievement, but there is substantial evidence that access to and use of computers and the Internet are changing the way teachers teach and students learn. If the introduction of technology has not had the impact on classrooms and schools that policymakers expected, the difficulty might relate more to their own misunderstanding of the conditions that facilitate success. Our intent in publishing this collection of stories is to respond to the cynics who have misguidedly cited Larry Cuban's findings as another reason for giving up on public schools and to enlighten policymakers about what impact telecommunications technologies can have on schools, teachers, and students when they create the right incentives and conditions.

IDENTIFYING AND IMPLEMENTING
THE CONDITIONS FOR SUCCESS

Each of our authors is operating under the belief that technology can play a critical role in the advancement of knowledge and in extending opportunities for learning. They are using technology to help students master academic content and deal with real-world problems. They are familiar with research and evaluation findings and are making use of studies that identify the conditions that are most likely to contribute to success. Both the teachers and students in their programs have become engaged and active learners. Strong leadership and the involvement of stakeholders—including parents and community leaders—are evident in all instances. Four of the principles that appear to be guiding their successful programs are summarized below.

Professional Development:
A Clinical and Collaborative Experience

Robert Tai and Eleanor Vernon Wilson share their experiences of working with teachers and prospective teachers in school districts surrounding the University of Virginia. Like Larry Cuban, they found many situations in which "the technology has fallen far short of addressing the hopes of educators and the sales pitches of technologists." However, they have an optimistic outlook. They suggest that the problems relating to *oversold and underused* have more to do with the type of professional development most teachers experience. They advocate contextual in-service programs that encourage preservice and experienced teachers to learn together in real classroom settings, and encourage teachers to use generative technology, which they describe as using the technology to create original materials that are responsive to statewide assessment requirements.

Randy Bell and Robert Tai pick up on the acknowledgment that the *oversold and underused* finding may have some validity. They cite the nearly universal access to educational technology and conclude: "Despite this unprecedented access to computers and the Internet, few teachers are using these technologies to anything close to their full instructional potential." Bell and Tai discovered what Larry Cuban found, that too many teachers use technology to teach the same content in the same manner they always have. Their argument is similar to that presented by Barbara Means (SRI International), which is that professional development relating to educational technology must be connected to the content and curricula offered by the school, system, and state. The preservice program they implement includes specialized educational technology courses and science methods courses in which content-based uses of technology are modeled. Bell and Tai also discuss the importance of having "teacher mentors" and describe how the new teachers and experienced teachers benefit from the collaborative experience.

State Leadership: Setting Standards and Promoting Local Entrepreneurship

James Eschenmann is working under conditions that are quite different from those that exist in the Ohio school district described by Pfundstein. Harrison County, West Virginia, is a relatively poor rural area that receives limited funds for the kinds of materials and services that can make a big difference in a school's success. There are many such communities in this state, and many depend on leadership and support from state officials. Eschenmann's school district and others throughout the state participated in a statewide comprehensive initiative aiming to raise the basic educational performance of schools and students. In 1991, the state launched its Basic Skills/Computer Education Program, which provided all schools with hardware and software, as well as professional development for all teachers. This program is now in its eleventh year and has been deemed successful by independent researchers and program evaluators. Although this was a well-orchestrated statewide program, individual schools and teachers were given considerable discretion as to how and where the computer-based instructional services would be conducted. As Eschenmann explains, the infusion of technology has improved student achievement, increased learning opportunities beyond school settings, increased students' desire to learn, and prepared graduates for the modern workplace. The two most plaguing problems have been persuading teachers who are set in their ways to change their teaching styles and the difficulty of providing rural schools with sufficient technical support.

Christine Richards works in a poor and rural school district in the north central portion of West Virginia. In spite of the conditions that are typically associated with poorly performing schools, Richards and her colleagues have been able to achieve a number of positive results. She attributes much of her school's success to the community's support and to the willingness of the parents to get involved. However, as Eschenmann also explains in his paper, much of the success in improving students' access to and use of learning technologies is attributed to leadership at the state level. West Virginia's Basic Skill/Computer Education Program provided all of the K–6 classrooms in the district with computers as well as software that was aligned with the state's instructional goals and objectives. Technology was adopted as a means of achieving higher reading and math scores. Following this successful program, the state adopted a second statewide technology initiative involving applications of advanced technologies to improve middle, junior high, and high school course offerings. Again, local schools were given considerable discretion in how they chose to implement the programs. In addition to citing data that demonstrate increased student performance, Richards refers to her own personal satisfaction at witnessing classrooms that seemed to treat students as moving on an assembly line change to classrooms that strive to engage students in lively cooperative settings.

Pioneering Local School Systems: Testbeds for the Future

Blake West describes how Kansas's Blue Valley Unified School District created the conditions that support and encourage teachers to use technology to improve and extend student learning. Success is not attributed to any statewide directive but to a well-designed and locally conceived professional development program. The programs were offered at different times and at a variety of locations. Peers (district teachers) who were familiar with the curriculum requirements taught the classes. The programs focused on teaching content and on the teaching skills required to be successful. The programs were influenced by research findings and reports of "best practices." West also points out that the professional development programs were fun. Blue Valley's professional development encouraged teachers in the direction of constructivist approaches and showed teachers how they could help students to explore, test hypotheses, and verify the validity of concepts through the use of technology. Students are encouraged to use the Internet in conducting scientific investigations and to analyze data sources, and many of the students provide the teachers and schools with the technical support for maintaining and operating computer-based programs. In addition, the school system makes use of technology integration specialists and cadres of technical support personnel who can quickly address problems with hardware and software.

Thomas Pfundstein is one of the individuals whose name surfaced whenever the editor discussed this project. After reading about his experience and accomplishments, one can understand why. While teaching in a well-heeled community and working in a technology-rich environment, teachers like this fellow can easily flourish. Nevertheless, he experiences some of the same frustrations and constraints that most other classroom teachers encounter. It's also evident that Pfundstein would succeed in schools and classrooms that have fewer computers and support services. Like some of the other authors, he is confronting many of the typical challenges: lack of time to prepare lessons that effectively integrate technology, rapid changes in the technology, lack of technical support, the fact that access to computers and the Internet can divert students to an interesting—but nonacademic—website, and making the necessary adjustments in teaching practices to fully maximize the benefits of Web-based learning. The fact that Pfundstein demonstrates a concern for research on teaching and learning and consistently measures his teaching performance on the basis of what his students have learned should give the reader a sense that he understands the values of technology—and, more so, the value of education.

Diane Reed is among those who recognize the contribution that Larry Cuban and others are making by questioning the impact of educational technology on schools and student achievement. However, she also agrees with those who have criticized his conclusions as premature. Reed works in an affluent school district and is involved in building a model for investigating and implementing uses of technology by providing the essential conditions for success. At the outset of her project, she addressed several conditions for success: ensuring universal access, providing sufficient time for teachers to practice and experiment, overall district-level planning, support, and leadership. As a first step in building a model program, Reed and her colleagues have engaged the support and involvement of the district's service providers, the technology firms and software providers. They have become active participants in addressing the question, "Why does technology work in some schools and not in others?" The model program is making use of the *enGauge* website, which provides a framework and assessment tool for understanding the systemwide factors that influence the effective use of educational technology. The program is also using the *LoTi Profile*, a measurement that helps determine a classroom teacher's capacity to use technology appropriately. The intent is to address the claim by Cuban that the availability of technology rarely changes the way teachers teach. This is another example of a district taking a more systematic approach and drawing upon the available body of research and reports on "best practices."

Teacher-Led Improvement Programs

Diane Bennett works as a technology coach at Mt. Juliet High School in Middle Tennessee about twenty minutes from Nashville. The school has had the benefit of additional resources provided by a grant from the Technology Literacy Challenge Fund. Although the state provides considerable leadership support, the school is more influenced by the guidelines provided by its local school improvement plan. Teachers are encouraged to develop their own lesson plans while they are being instructed in ways to integrate technology. The lesson plans are expected to address the state's curriculum standards, to engage students, and to use technology to support student-centered learning. The professional development program, the collaborating exercises involving teams of teachers, and the support from an on-site technology coach are models that most districts should consider. The teachers meet in reflection and collection sessions and discuss what worked and what didn't. Although all of their successful lessons are shared on the network, teachers do not have as much time as students do to experiment with networked resources and services. As Bennett points out, teachers enjoy the lesson plan workshops because they are able to make choices and collaborate with other teachers in the group, which is limited to ten to twelve teachers. She agrees with Cuban by commenting that "much needs to be done" and that in addition to providing on-site professional development, social, political, and organizational changes must occur.

Mary Haney and Elaine Wilkins work at the Ida B. Wells Academy in Memphis, Tennessee. They describe the school as serving some one hundred seventh and eighth grade students who have been referred to the school because they lack academic success and have been unsuccessful in traditional school settings. The school's program reflects Howard Gardner's theory of multiple intelligences, which recognizes eight distinct types of learning.[3] Technology and collaborative learning are important elements of the school's curriculum. Technology is taught as a subject and is infused into the entire school curriculum. The school benefited from a Technology Literacy Challenge Fund grant, which enabled it to place ten computers in each core subject classroom and to employ a technology coach who leads or mentors a team of teachers. The teachers are trained to integrate technology into all subject areas. The key to the success of this program seems to have less to do with the number of computers—the school has many—and more to do with the team approach that has emerged from the professional development program. Teachers admit that most of the school's computers have been underused, but they insist that the situation is changing. There is evidence that the students are more engaged and that their academic performance is improving. The Ida B. Wells Academy is one of the many examples of a program that could be replicated by other schools in other regions of the country.

State and local policymakers must be able to identify the resources that teachers and students need to be successful. They should also encourage their school administrators and their educational technology program directors and coordinators to identify and adapt successful and proven practices. Educational technologies have become a critical part of the mix of resources that will improve and extend learning. No one really doubts the importance of ensuring that all schools have access to the Internet and Web-based educational services. The challenge has moved from ensuring access to ensuring that available technologies support standards-based educational reform and improvement.

• *State and local education policies should reflect research and experience in creating learner-centered environments for teachers and students.* Teachers who are teaching with or without the assistance of technology need not operate from a clearly defined theory of instruction. They must, however, understand the conditions under which learning takes place. Researchers have long recognized that there are multiple types of learning and, more recently, that there are multiple intelligences (Gardner, 1983, 1991). Researchers have also acknowledged the value of creating learner-centered environments that enable teachers to monitor individual student performance (National Research Council, 2000). Although the authors in this volume do not go out of their way to cite psychological foundations and research findings that influence their approaches for addressing the needs of low- or high-achieving students, undoubtedly they are aware of the best practices and lessons learned. Their experiments are well grounded. There is also awareness that the availability of technology is having an influence on what is taught, how the technology is enhancing different types of learning, and how the technology is helping them to keep track of individual progress and academic achievement.

Researchers are continuing to shed light on the impact of technology on different types of learning experiences, and many educational practitioners—including those who report their experiences in this publication—are in a position to provide policymakers with the conditions for success. We hope that their experiences demonstrate how all schools can make effective use of educational technology to improve the performance of their teachers and students.

NOTES

1. *Washington Post,* 16 September 2001, W15.
2. Our definitions of *educational technology* and *telecommunications services* refer to a wide range of technologies that support education, including

computers, CD-ROMS, handheld wireless devices, and Internet and Web-based services. For the purposes of this initiative, we are excluding the use and impact of broadcast and cable television.

3. In his recent book, *Multiple Intelligences and Instructional Technology— A Manual for Every Mind*, Walter McKenzie explains how to apply instructional technologies to nine different intelligences and help all children succeed. McKenzie leverages Howard Gardner's evolving work on multiple intelligences, providing a strong and logical foundation for using technology to enliven current lesson plans and build a repertoire of flexible teaching methods. This book provides examples that support multidisciplinary and special needs teaching and learning.

REFERENCES

Gardner, Howard. (1983). *Frames of mind: The theory of multiple intelligences.* New York: Basic Books.

Gardner, Howard. (1991). *The unschooled mind: How children think and how schools should teach.* New York: Basic Books.

National Research Council, Commission on Behavioral and Social Sciences and Education (2000). *How people learn: Brain, mind, experience, and school: Expanded edition.* Washington, D.C.: National Academy Press.

BEYOND COMPREHENSION: ELEMENTARY EDUCATION AND GENERATIVE TECHNOLOGY

Robert H. Tai and Eleanor Vernon Wilson

Curry School of Education, University of Virginia

INTRODUCTION

One at a time, the students moved to the front of the crowded computer room, slowly, with hesitation and a little trepidation. A little boy picks his way through the students sitting on the floor at the front of the room. "Hi," he says. A whisper from his tutor prompts him, "Say your name." The little boy says, "Casey. This is my presentation on sharks." He quickly and easily clicks through his presentation slides, narrating each item, and periodically noting when a misspelled word appeared on a slide. His presentation ends with an enthusiastic round of applause from his classmates, his mother, his tutor, and a few other interested observers. He smiles and shyly picks his way back through his classmates sitting on the floor. He is nine years old, and this was his first technology-assisted presentation. We pause to think about the implications of a fourth grader expressing his thoughts and ideas using a software package that would allow him to show what he means as he explains.

Although computer-based presentations are exciting to watch, the novelty soon wears off and we are left with pedagogical implications related to their use. Technology has been incorporated to a certain extent in many classrooms in the United States, yet criticisms have quickly emerged about the quality and quantity of educational improvement these innovations have brought about. Among these critics is Larry Cuban, whose research suggests that technology has fallen far short of addressing the hopes of educators and the sales pitches of technologists. He states in his book, *Oversold and Underused*:

> Although promoters of new technologies often spout the rhetoric of fundamental change, few have pursued deep and comprehensive changes in the existing system of schooling. The introduction of information technologies into schools over the past two decades has achieved neither the transformation of teaching and learning nor the productivity gains that a reform coalition of corporate executives, public officials, parents, academics, and educators have sought. (Cuban, 2001, p. 195)

By now, it is well known that in our haste to impose technology on classrooms, teachers, and schools in general, many significant areas necessary for successful implementation have been overlooked, thus impeding the hope for educational reforms. Two of these important areas are pedagogy and professional development. What do these changes in teaching options mean in terms of learning for students and how can these changes be implemented in a manner that will improve the efficacy of teachers?

First, we turn to the options for learning and teaching of elementary school children. We provide examples of the work of students using software; we label this adaptive use of technology *generative technology*, drawing from the term *generative knowledge* coined by John Dewey. According to David Perkins, "[Dewey] wanted education to emphasize knowledge with rich ramifications in the lives of learners. Knowledge worth understanding" (Perkins, 1993, pp. 27–34). Perkins argues that this *knowledge worth understanding* stems from the possibilities for this knowledge to transfer from the specific learning situations in which the student first encounters this knowledge to subsequent real-life situations in which the student may find this knowledge useful as he or she makes decisions. We provide details and examples of what we see as technology worth understanding, that is, technology that can be transferred from situation to situation and be appropriate and useful, thereby contributing to learning.

Second, we focus on possibilities for long-term change through professional development for classroom teachers. Our model proposes that we shift from traditional professional development that draws teachers out of their own classrooms to "contextual in-service" that brings professional development into the classroom, in our case, through working with these teachers' own students.

TECHNOLOGY WORTH UNDERSTANDING

This project began with a teacher education faculty member's efforts to put together a technology-based teaching methods course for preservice elementary school teachers. She coalesced the technological needs of two schools, a lower elementary school (grades K–4) and an upper elementary school (grades 5–6), with her vision for an elementary teacher education program, designing an after-school program in which preservice teachers tutored elementary school students in the use of two software applications, a presentation package and a website design package. Under this program, the elementary students learned to apply technological skills by creating presentations and websites on topics in science and social studies, and the preservice teachers learned firsthand how to teach children how to use technology; ultimately, elementary school teachers would see their students using technology and would have technology-capable students bringing their newly gained expertise back to their classes. The schools requested that topics for these presentations be related to state-mandated objectives in science and social studies.

The K–4 elementary school houses 260 students, with roughly 45 students in two classes in third grade and 60 students in three classes in fourth grade. Built in 1924, the school was recently renovated and serves a diverse mix of children from various socioeconomic and racial backgrounds. The upper elementary school serves the entire community of 40,000 residents. This school has 600 students from a wide array of backgrounds with a student population much like that of the grades K–4 elementary school. The upper elementary has a one-level open classroom design reminiscent of the 1970s.

The technology available in both schools consists of one computer classroom containing twenty computers and one or two computers in each teacher's classroom. The newest of the computers are from four to five generations old. Implementing change in a class such as this presented challenges for the preservice teachers and instructors and illustrated the hurdles faced by classroom teachers. In addition, the computers in both schools are Macintoshes, and the preservice students' introduction to computer technology was based solely on PCs, another issue for all involved. The software packages used by the students in the after-school project ran slowly and at times "locked-up." Yet the students and their preservice teachers and tutors persevered and produced many projects over the course of eight weeks. The children began by learning how to use the presentation software package. The result would be a multiple-panel presentation on a science or social studies topic of each child's choosing. We have chosen several examples of the children's work to illustrate the kinds of projects created in this class.

Casey is a fourth grader, and his presentation on sharks began with the title "Sharks in the Ocean" spiraling onto the screen, followed by a byline with Casey's name. The next slide transitioned on to the screen and was headed with the question, "What is a shark?" followed by a series of scientific facts about the history of sharks in general. The next slide focused on the spined pygmy shark and was accompanied by a list of facts and a cartoon illustrating its size relative to a scuba diver. The next slide was about the whale shark and had the same format of facts with a cartoon showing relative sizes of the sharks to the same scuba diver. In all, Casey had created a nine-slide presentation that included graphics and text describing several characteristics of each of six different sharks. The presentation took advantage of the animation, sound effects, and background options available through the presentation software. Casey's final slide contained a link to a website that he used as a reference for his presentation.

Therin is a fifth grader, and his presentation focused on volcanoes. He began with the question: "What is a volcano?" After describing the definition in both text and pictures, he went on to provide some interesting facts. After this introduction, he continued by describing four specific scientific designations of volcanic eruptions: Plinian, Hawaiian, Strombolian, and Vulcanian. These terms are drawn from both historical and geographical references and to the novice volcanologist would have very little meaning. However, Therin also included pictures illustrating and text describing each of these categories. The Plinian eruptions slide showed a wide river of lava and the caption, "Large landslide of lava that destroys everything in its path." The Hawaiian eruption slide showed lava spouting from a conical land mass and then flowing away in stream of molten earth. This slide had the caption, "Fountain of fire with rivers of liquid lava." The textual and graphical descriptions continued for the other two types of eruptions, and the presentation ended with a summary slide defining eruptions. Therin also used a highly appropriate slide template with a black background that matched well with the overall theme of the presentation.

These initial presentations typically made use of the various options for animations, backgrounds, and sounds. The use of these options opens the door for students to push the envelope of possibilities for their future work. After the presentations using the software were completed, the children moved on to website design. They were introduced to the concept of webbing ideas, drawing initial diagrams for their proposed projects prior to beginning their work.

James Madison was the subject for a website designed by Kahlique and headed by the title, "Who Is James Madison?" above a portrait of the fourth president. The text began with an introduction that included some general facts about President Madison and a welcome to the website. Scrolling down the site, fourth grader Kahlique next had a section that provided some interesting information about Madison's childhood. He also included a link to a website that provided even more details. The next section of the website was entitled "His Presidency." This section included two paintings of battles from the War of 1812, and the text spoke generally of Madison's relationship to Thomas Jefferson and the fact that he played some role in the American Revolution. The form of the text and its apparent lack of connection to the paintings left very little doubt that Kahlique was in fourth grade. However, the navigation links placed at the ends of the sections on Madison's childhood and his presidency also give the impression that Kahlique was beginning to master the skills of putting together a well-formed website. Included in the section on Madison's presidency was a link to another website on the Internet with further information. Kahlique's site ended with an acknowledgment of all those who had helped him put the site together.

"Kelsey's Virginia Page" began with a really big number, "6,992,045," the population of the state. Kelsey was in the fourth grade, and in her Web page she focused on the geographical and geological aspects of Virginia. She included a concise yet fairly detailed description of the four diverse geological regions of the state of Virginia. She listed the four regions as Tidewater, Piedmont, Ridge and Valley, and Allegheny Highlands. Beside simply naming these four regions, Kelsey included geological descriptions of land formations and bodies of water, while also noting important cities located within each of these regions. The website included a picture of a Civil War era battlefield cannon and concluded with a series of links to various websites with more information about the state. The site was thoughtfully put together using colorful text to emphasize specific words and phrases. The cannon stands as a quirky reminder of Virginia's role in the "war between the states."

Susan was a fifth grader, and her website described the life of Maggie Walker, an African American businesswoman who became the first woman to be a bank president in the 1920s. Susan's website included some important navigational options that allowed the reader to move from section to section. She included four sections: Childhood, Adult Life, Why She Is Important, and Death. Susan created a navigation bar at the top of her Web page that listed these four sections. Each word was actually a hotlink to the corresponding section at some other point on the website. Clicking on these hotlinks would skip the reader lower on the Web page to the sections associated with these links. Once the readers had completed a section, Susan included "To Top" return links that would allow the reader to return to the top of the website. The navigational links not only allowed the reader to move freely about the website but also put to use the nonlinear property of website design. In addition, Susan's website included two black-and-white photographs. One is a portrait of Maggie Walker showing a serene middle-aged woman with short wavy hair in a modest dress. Her eyes seem to stare off into space, giving no hint of the hardships that Susan described about her life in the text. The other photograph shows Ms. Walker standing in front of the Saint Luke Penny Savings Bank. Her right hand gently rests on the shoulder of a young girl whose head only comes up to Ms. Walker's waist. Seven little boys sit on the curb in a line facing the camera. A subtle yet telling feature of this snapshot of Ms. Walker posing with eight young children is the expression captured on her face, a look of contentment and happiness. The pictures were essential to Ms. Walker's story, a story that would seem to be fiction if not for these photographs. Susan used these pictures as hotlink buttons to another website with even more information about Maggie Lena Walker.

For these five students and the other twenty students participating in this project, presentation and website design software is now a tool to give form and function to their ideas. These examples of student work were not without flaws—there were links that didn't work on first, second, or even third attempts, for example—but the fact remains that the third, fourth, fifth, and sixth graders who were given access to, tutoring with, and guidance in using this generative technology now possess the skills to express their ideas in a manner not limited to the traditional "paper and pencil" modes of expression. The presentations reflect learning on several different levels, incorporating both inductive and deductive reasoning skills, and they reflect interpretative abilities that are key to the development of critical thinking skills. Yet even these hopeful examples of generative technology begun with the children may eventually fade if a teacher-based infrastructure is not put in place to support efforts enabling classroom teachers to implement integration of these strategies in their teaching.

POSSIBILITIES FOR LONG-TERM CHANGE

This section describes our model for in-service teacher professional development so that you can begin to form an image of the possibilities. We then provide the details of our current efforts to implement this model given the resources and limitations of our specific situation.

Efforts at integrating technology and education have focused on procuring hardware and software for schools and then encouraging, cajoling, and even requiring teachers to apply these tools in their teaching. The approach is akin to buying a hammer and then searching around for things to pound down. The results are usually not very useful, and they are often counterproductive. The approach of technology procurement ignores teachers and their needs and centers on the purchasing of technology to be injected into schools, often without the necessary educational support for teachers. That this effort is clearly meeting with failure is the argument underlying Cuban's book. Cooper and Bull continue: "Those who identify meaningful uses of technology relevant to their disciplines do not have to be coerced through legislation or standards to include them in their courses." (1997, p. 105).

The necessary and appropriate professional development to enable teachers to successfully integrate technological applications in their teaching is sorely lacking in many cases. However, we do not mean to imply that the solution to successful technology integration is simply more professional development in its current form. We are proposing a rethinking of the current notion of professional development from the traditional in-service form that pulls teachers out of classrooms into a format that allows teachers to work in their classrooms with their own students while learning new skills.

A model of "contextual in-service" provides teachers with an experience that allows them to consider the challenges of their classrooms while having access to those most knowledgeable about the technology on hand. It is not enough merely to show teachers, apart from the students, how to teach something using some kind of technological tool intended to "promote" a child's understanding. It is not enough to merely teach the students in "push-in teaching" scenarios where expert technology teachers take over the teaching duties from regular classroom teachers while the regular teachers tend to other duties. We believe that to catalyze long-term change, we must have regular classroom teachers in regular classrooms with students present, all working with technology-proficient teachers. The students would be learning how to use generative technology to do projects, while their regular classroom teachers would be involved in both learning how to use the generative technology and helping and sometimes learning from their students. The advantages are numerous. However, most important, the classroom teachers have the experience of seeing their own students working with new technology in productive and useful ways. The "contextual in-service" model sets up the opportunity for the students to learn from expert technology teachers and their own regular classroom teachers simultaneously. The technology teachers would provide support and expertise, while the classroom teachers would provide instructional insight tailored to the students they are very familiar with. The long-term change comes from the regular classroom teachers, who have had the opportunity to see the generative technology actually work in their own classrooms with their own students while they have gained the skills and confidence to use this technology. Given such encouragement and experience with new technology, regular classroom teachers would then begin to see generative technology as a curricular option, and once regular classroom teachers include technology in their teaching repertoire, the seeds for long-term change have been planted.

The elementary-school student projects discussed in detail in the previous section are examples of the work students participating in this project are capable of creating. An in-school, "push-in" program in cooperation with an elementary science teaching methods class was introduced in the fall of 2001 and has met with encouraging reviews. This in-school science program provides preservice student teachers with the opportunity to design and to teach science lessons to small groups of five to seven students. Classroom teachers were extremely supportive of this approach, and our plan is to coalesce the educational technology instruction in the after-school program with the push-in teaching methods program to form the contextual in-service model discussed previously in this section. Implementation of our in-service teacher education model began in the fall of 2002.

CONCLUSION

Although we realize that the points made in Larry Cuban's book are based on good evidence, we believe that the state of disuse and disarray that Cuban describes in educational technology is steadily changing into a new state of excitement and hope. Clearly, the advantages of technology have shown themselves to be greater than the initial costs that we must pay to gain the requisite skills and confidence to work smoothly and effectively. As educators, we should also consider the consequences of ignoring educational technology. Would our students have the skills and the background to compete with their technologically adept peers? Would they find themselves lost in an unfamiliar world that would expect them to search the Internet for a URL where they can download the proper software to view PDF versions of documents? Given that technology and the ability to use it are essential for every student, then as a matter of course, the presence of technology and the ability to use it are essential for every teacher.

We also firmly believe that the complexities of effective technological instructional use cannot be simply addressed by conventional, often superficial, in-service training for classroom teachers, but instead should be focused on long-term daily generative integration in classroom instruction. Such instruction will provide teachers with the necessary tools, self-confidence, and motivation to incorporate these strategies for the betterment of children in schools. The days of drill and practice are over. We are now in a time of flux and change, when what we as students knew and what as teachers assume is far from the realities of technological expertise and possibility faced by our students. We believe that educational technology through appropriate professional development is taking a foothold in everyday educational practice; it is the obligation of all educators to ensure that such practice continues.

REFERENCES

Cooper, James M., & Bull, Glen L. (1997). Technology and teacher education: Past practice and recommended directions. *Action in Teacher Education, XIX* (2), 97–106.

Cuban, Larry. (2001). *Oversold and underused: Computers in the classroom.* Cambridge, MA: Harvard University Press.

Perkins, David. (1993, Fall). Teaching for understanding. *American Educator,* 27–34.

2

TRANSFORMING SCIENCE
INSTRUCTION WITH TECHNOLOGY

Randy L. Bell and Robert H. Tai

Curry School of Education, University of Virginia

INTRODUCTION

The last two decades have brought about an unprecedented prolifera-
tion of computer technologies in public schools. This has certainly been
the case within the schools of the central Virginia region, and in particular, in the schools in which our preservice science teachers complete
their student teaching. In Albemarle County Schools, for instance, the
ratio of students to computers has decreased from 9.5:1 to 4.4:1 during
the past five years alone (Fisher, personal communication). The same
trend can be seen in our local schools and classrooms with regard to Internet access. Today, every school in Albemarle County Public Schools
has access to the Internet; each individual classroom is wired to the Internet with four hard-wired connections (Fisher, personal communication). Despite this unprecedented access to computers and the Internet,
few teachers are using these technologies to anything close to their full
instructional potential.

During the past three years, we have begun to mitigate this problem
through our science teacher education program. These efforts have resulted in three important changes in the way we teach our students
about technology. First, we now incorporate instructional technology

more consistently throughout the science education program. Second, we promote a clearer vision of how technology can be used to support rather than supplant appropriate content and pedagogy. Third, and most important, we now model instructional technology innovation and use in all of our science education courses.

Although our efforts have focused on our preservice science teachers' vision and skills regarding instructional uses of technology, we have begun to observe positive effects on the mentor teachers who work with our students. This chapter describes the initial success of our program, illustrating the ways in which our student teachers have put technology to use in their teaching and the ways that they have improved the manner in which their mentor teachers view and use technology.

DEFINING THE ISSUE

There is currently much discussion concerning the "digital divide," but teacher and student access to technology is likely to become less of an issue as computer technology continues to become more affordable and ubiquitous. The new digital divide will be a *didactic* digital divide. As Kathleen Fulton, a policy analyst for the U.S. Office of Technology Assessment, suggests, students in wealthier schools will be more likely to experience the empowering kinds of educational uses than those in less affluent schools (Fulton, personal comunication). The primary issue will become whether this ubiquitous resource is being used to its full advantage in classrooms around the United States. In *Oversold and Underused*, Larry Cuban presents a compelling and well-documented argument that, although educational technologies have been widely promoted for their capability to transform instruction, most have not lived up to their full potential. Cuban reports that even in schools located in the technology-rich Silicon Valley, most teachers do not use any form of computer technology for instruction (Cuban, 2001). And those teachers who do use computers tend to use them as word processors and glorified reference books. At best, teachers seem to be using technology to teach the same content in the same manner they always have. At worst, unused computers are collecting dust and taking up space in classrooms.

Many educators and public officials are scratching their heads and wondering, "What has caused this state of affairs?" Yet this situation is not really surprising. Clearly, technology will not transform instruction if teachers are not using it. And teachers will not use technology if they cannot envision how it will enhance instruction and student learning. What little professional development is offered in educational technology often is not connected to the content and does not model innovative styles of teaching that can take advantage of technology's unique features.

Educating practicing teachers on the effective and appropriate uses of technology requires a massive commitment of time and money from school districts. But even with a firm commitment by schools to apply technology, research on professional development indicates that changing teachers' instructional practice is extremely difficult. Although, according to Cuban, most teachers included in his study used the computer extensively at home (Cuban, 2001), teachers tend to teach the way they were taught, and most have never seen technology used in an innovative and imaginative way.

One possible solution to this dilemma lies in the fact that, on the average, one-tenth of the teacher workforce turns over every year. Thus, over the course of five years, a large number of teachers will be new to the profession. Teachers currently entering the workforce in many cases have quite literally grown up during the Information Age. A beginning teacher in 2001 at the age of twenty-four would have been born in 1977 and would have been a high school student from 1991 to 1995, a college student from 1995 to 1999, and in either the workforce or post-graduate studies from 1999 to the present. It is likely that as far as these beginning teachers can remember, computers have always been the most common way to compose term papers. They probably do not remember a time when "getting something off the Net" was not a possibility.

As the new teacher workforce becomes more and more technology capable, innovative uses of technology will enter the classroom not by way of a top-down model of professional development, but through a more grassroots model of hiring technology-capable teachers who can then begin to influence their peers by modeling innovative technology use and acting as resources.

Preservice teachers over the next decade will be completing their formal education during a time when more and more technology is being used in content courses at schools and colleges. These preservice teachers potentially will be exposed to instructional uses of technology. However, relying on content courses alone to model appropriate educational uses of technology is risky. As Cuban's work suggests, most professors and teachers are slow to adopt technology into their classroom instruction beyond superficial applications. Some science classes provide examples of the use of instructional technology, but these uses might not be considered "best practice." Preparing preservice teachers to integrate technology into their instruction, then, becomes an important objective for teacher educators. The responsibility for modeling instructional uses of technology is likely to rest firmly on our shoulders.

The Curry School of Education at the University of Virginia is recognized as a leader in technology integration. Throughout the teacher education program, preservice teachers are encouraged to learn and teach with technologies and to reflect on ways in which technologies can improve teaching and learning within their content areas. This is especially true for the secondary science education program, which has undergone significant revision during the last three years. The program now includes specialized educational technology courses and science methods courses in which content-based uses of technologies are modeled. Preservice teachers are encouraged to use readily available emerging technologies and to reflect critically on the uses of educational technologies in teaching science. Although it is still too early to assess the full impact of this revised program, we have begun to collect data on how our teachers are using their technology skills and knowledge in the classroom. The preliminary evidence indicates that they are using technology in substantial ways to enhance science instruction, despite the fact that there is no program requirement for students to use technology at all in their student teaching experience.

We collected a combination of observational and interview data to characterize how our preservice teachers were using technology in their instruction during their student teaching. The fourteen participating students represented one cohort in our science teacher education program. Ten of these students were in the fifth year of their five-year program that culminates in a dual B.A./M.T. (masters in teaching), as well as earning each of them a license to teach science in their respective content areas. The other four students had previously earned a B.A. or B.S. in science and were in the second year of an accelerated two-year program that culminates with the M.T. and a teaching license.

During the fall of 2001, our team made more than eighty visits to our preservice teachers' classrooms to observe their instruction and their use of technology. At the conclusion of the student teaching experience, we interviewed each preservice teacher, along with his or her mentor teacher, to characterize the impact of technology on the instruction of both the student teacher and the mentor. The interview and observation data were then summarized and combined to create the characterizations of technology use and impact reported in the following sections.

When analyzing the use of technology among our students, we chose to categorize their technology use into three groups: noninstructional uses, instructional uses, and instructional innovations. Noninstructional uses focus on task efficiency and record keeping. For example, spreadsheet applications to record grades or word processing applications to write tests or lessons plans would be considered noninstructional uses. Instructional uses engage students in activities in which technology is used to support more traditional methods of instruction. For example, using presentation software to display lecture notes and using the Internet as a reference source in place of an encyclopedia are instructional uses of technology. Instructional innovation takes advantage of technology to move beyond typical classroom experiences. For example, using presentation software as a means for students to create representations of their ideas in a rich and complex manner and using data gathered from the Internet to answer research questions posed by the students are instructional innovations. In the following section, we discuss all three categories of use among our preservice teachers, focusing primarily on instructional uses and instructional innovations.

NONINSTRUCTIONAL USES:
THE NEW BASIC SKILLS

Like Cuban, we found noninstructional uses of technology to be pervasive among our preservice teachers. All fourteen of our preservice teachers used technology to keep track of attendance and grades and to create lesson plans, worksheets, and tests. Unlike the teachers in Cuban's investigation, however, none of our students stopped at this level of technology usage. Rather, 100 percent of our preservice teachers found ways to integrate technology into their instructional practice, as described in the following sections.

INSTRUCTIONAL USES: TECHNOLOGY TO SUPPORT TRADITIONAL PRACTICE

We classified a small majority of our preservice science teachers as technology users. In total, eight of the fourteen preservice teachers (57 percent) used technology during their student teaching experiences in ways that supported conventional instructional approaches. Typically, students in their classes used the Internet to collect information about science topics or used technology-enhanced data collection devices to augment traditional laboratory activities.

The practices of two preservice teachers, Erin and Tony, exemplify our definition of instructional uses of technology.

Erin

Erin taught biology in a mid-sized high school that services a rural population of 1,200 students. The school had one computer lab containing twenty-five computers. Because scheduling computer time was an issue, Erin commented in her interview that this was an insufficient number of computers for a school of this size. In addition, the computer in her mentor teacher's classroom had the capability to be connected to a television monitor so that it could be used for demonstration purposes. Yet the monitor had never been connected to the computer until Erin took on this responsibility.

Despite these and other challenges, Erin managed to include a considerable amount of technology in her classroom instruction. During a series of lessons involving the use of optical microscopes, Erin used a digital microscope connected to a computer (which she had been introduced to in her science methods class) to demonstrate for students the proper procedures for making wet-mount slides, differentiating living objects from inanimate objects (such as air bubbles), and focusing the microscope on microorganisms. Erin used this new technology to facilitate traditional laboratory procedures. However, in her interview Erin related an interesting episode resulting from her use of the digital microscope. One day a student with learning disabilities, Ben, brought a sample of stream water into class for extra credit. Serendipitously, this sample contained several hydra, tiny organisms the class was studying at the time. Erin and Ben were able to show the structure of the hydra with the electronic microscope and even captured video sequences of a hydra feeding and undergoing asexual reproduction. Because of his efforts, Ben received a good deal of positive reinforcement from Erin and his classmates. This resulted in a marked improvement in his classroom behavior and his course grades for the balance of the semester.

Erin also used a WebQuest she had developed on the topic of forensic science.[1] The WebQuest presented a murder mystery for her students to solve by applying scientific methodology to clues and data they located on the Web. This lesson had been originally developed without the use of technology, but Erin created the WebQuest to update the lesson and make it more interesting to her students.

Erin's success with applying technology in her student teaching experience had a significant impact on her mentor teacher's (Shannon's) attitudes toward instructional technology. Before Erin's arrival, Shannon had not even bothered to connect her classroom computer to a demonstration monitor. When she observed Erin's success with the digital microscope, she decided to purchase one to use in the future. In addition, Shannon had taught the same forensic science lesson in the past without using the WebQuest Erin employed. After observing her students' intensity and high degree of engagement with Erin's WebQuest, Shannon says she now plans to include it in her own lessons in the future. She also plans to search for WebQuests she could adapt for other lessons.

Erin introduced Shannon to a website containing interesting animations that illustrate concepts of evolution. Given that topics on evolution were to be taught after Erin's student teaching had concluded, Shannon decided to use these animations on her own when she tackled this unit in the subsequent semester.

Tony

One of the content areas in which a number of new tools for instructional technology have been developed is physics. Tony was a physics student teacher at the only public high school of a small city with an urban/suburban population of nearly 40,000. The high school has a diverse enrollment of more than 1,200 students. The technology available was fairly typical, with one computer in each classroom and two dedicated computer classrooms, each containing twenty computers.

Tony taught four junior-/senior-level physics classes. Although he did not use technology extensively throughout his student teaching experience, one occasion stood out. He designed a lesson on simple machines that incorporated calculator-based force probes. Typically, laboratory lessons of this nature are carried out with spring scales that are fairly inaccurate and at times inconsistent. Tony believed that he could avoid some of these problems by using the more robust force probes and at the same time give his students some exposure to applications of technology.

The lesson required the students to assemble the various parts of a calculator-based force probe to measure the changes in applied forces to three different simple machine setups. In the first setup, students measured the forces required to lift a 500-gram mass with a lever, with the mass and fulcrum at various positions on the lever. In the second setup, students measured the force required to lift a 500-gram mass with different combinations of pulleys. The third setup involved pulling a 500-gram mass up an inclined plane at various angles. In each of these laboratory setups, the students were required to physically manipulate actual simple machines, giving them a hands-on sense of the devices, while using the force probe to take measurements. The technology in this instance facilitated the data collection and gave students the opportunity to get both a physical understanding of the simple machines and a quantitative analysis of the forces. They could compare their qualitative observations while the data were collected and recorded by the calculator-based measurement tool.

Tony taught in a classroom setting where his mentor teacher could be considered a technology user. Throughout the semester, she occasionally used graphing calculators and probes, so the students in these classes were already familiar with these tools and did not need to be instructed in their use. Tony took the initiative with this lesson and integrated the technology so that the students could focus more on the concept of mechanical advantage and less on experimental error. In Tony's case, the mentor teacher and Tony used technology in similar ways, so Tony did not have a marked influence on his mentor teacher's level of technology integration.

INSTRUCTIONAL INNOVATIONS: CHALLENGE OF CREATIVITY

Our observation and interview data indicated that nearly half of the preservice teachers used technology in creative ways to transform the science curriculum during their student teaching experiences. For these students, technology provided a vehicle for innovation and creative approaches to teaching science concepts. The practices of Vance and Erica were typical of many of these preservice teachers and illustrate instructional technology innovations that push beyond the bounds of traditional teaching methods.

Vance

Vance student taught at the only high school in a small town with a population of 10,000. The student enrollment is nearly 800. This school is typical of most small communities; it serves all the students in the surrounding community and has a fairly diverse student population.

During his student teaching placement, Vance taught three classes of ninth-grade honors biology, with enrollments between twenty and twenty-two students. Block scheduling allowed for periods of up to one hour and forty-five minutes. Technology was perhaps more available at this school than in most. In addition to the typical one computer per classroom and dedicated computer labs, the school had ten desktop computers on portable carts, which could be checked out for extended periods of time.

We observed Vance teaching on several occasions. In two-thirds of these instances, he was making use of instructional technology. In one instance, Vance brought to class two microscopes in addition to those typically used in the classroom. His grandfather, who had trained as a physician during the early part of the twentieth century, had owned one of these microscopes. The second microscope was an electronic microscope introduced to Vance during his science teaching methods course. This inexpensive microscope was connected to a computer and allows the user to record both still images and short movies that could be viewed and stored on the computer. Vance's purpose was to give his students the opportunity to compare and contrast, not just obvious physical differences, but differences in performance. Clearly, the electronic microscope had some distinct advantages, but it also possessed limitations. Vance's goal for the lesson was for students to discover the limitations and advancements of microscope technology spanning nearly a century.

In another set of lessons, Vance's mentor teacher had introduced the use of a CD-ROM-based tutorial. This program was a traditional use of instructional technology, but Vance took this opportunity to introduce the use of a presentation software program that allowed students to illustrate and animate their ideas in complex ways. Taking the time to introduce the program, Vance allowed the novelty to wear off during a "fun" project that allowed the students to explore the various tools available in the program while presenting something of their own choosing. Once the students had presented their start-up projects, Vance assigned them the task of presenting their understanding of various types of cells, the organelles within these cells, and the functions of these organelles. Using action buttons, several students developed nonlinear presentations that allowed them to show more detailed information on certain concepts as questions arose from the audience of fellow students. The presentation software gave students the opportunity to be not merely receivers of information but generators of knowledge.

In these two instances, Vance took instructional use of technology beyond typical applications, giving his students the opportunity to evaluate, synthesize, and create their own understandings. Vance's mentor teacher had over thirty years of experience and was just beginning to implement technology applications in his instruction, primarily in a supplemental fashion. The CD-ROM tutorials were his first attempt at technology integration, and he was excited about the possibility of having his students learn using this alternate form of drill and practice. His vision of technology in the classroom setting centered primarily on replacing or supplementing his past practices with technological applications. Vance's approach of having students use presentation software to synthesize the ideas and concepts being presented to them through the tutorial program altered his mentor teacher's vision of content-based instructional practice and taught his mentor teacher a new and exciting application. The mentor teacher voiced his resolve to continue to use both the combination of the tutorial and the presentation software in his classes in the future.

Erica

Erica taught earth science in a high school located in a small town with 600 students drawn from the town and surrounding rural areas. In her classroom, there was one computer connected to a television monitor for demonstration purposes. This situation was actually rather unusual, given that few other classrooms in that school had this capacity. Although some computers were available in the library for instructional use, there were no monitors connected for purposes of demonstration in the dedicated computer classrooms.

Erica's mentor teacher, Becky, took advantage of the computer and monitor in her classroom to present her class notes using a software presentation program and to show images from the Web. The mentor teacher also taught her students to use presentation software and assigned them to report on their class projects at the end of the school year. Erica chose not to use the computer and monitor setup to present her class notes, favoring the overhead projector. However, she made extensive use of a virtual planetarium software program, which can show the positions and motions of celestial objects from any position on Earth at various times of the year. This program had been introduced to her during her science teaching methods course. She used the software to demonstrate how to find constellations, star clusters, galaxies, and planets; to teach about the negative effects of light pollution; and to teach the concept of circumpolar stars and the precession of the celestial poles.

Erica was impressed with the software's capability of allowing students to see for themselves these abstract concepts, which are typically presented only in text. She found that her students were highly engaged and very much enjoyed using the program—so much so that students often came up to her after class, eager to continue using the program on their own, despite the overcrowding around the single computer.

This level of student engagement was also reflected in other uses of technology Erica introduced through her instruction. For example, when she used a spreadsheet and M&M candies to teach a unit on probability, her students spent much of the time helping each other, as they developed formulas and graphed data while exploring the color distributions of the candies.

In addition, Erica introduced some advanced features of a presentation software program to her students. Erica's efforts catalyzed her students to go beyond mere simple linear presentations that mimicked overhead slides. The success of Erica's technology integration greatly impressed not only her mentor teacher but also the entire science department. Erica's use of the planetarium software initiated a major change in the science department's approach to its current curriculum. The department has now purchased nearly two-dozen copies of the program, and Becky has begun to rewrite the curriculum to take advantage of the capabilities of the software to help students visualize complex and abstract concepts. The science department also decided to develop an entire unit on graphs and graphing using the capabilities of the spreadsheet program introduced by Erica.

SUMMARIZING OUR THOUGHTS

Cuban reported some computer use in the technology-rich Silicon Valley in high school English and social studies classes and little to no use in math and science classes. In addition, he found that when computers were used in classrooms, they were typically used for typing up assignments, working on reports, and searching the Internet. Cuban reached the disheartening conclusion that, taken as a whole, computers have been oversold and underused in education.

The results of our work paint a more promising picture. Six of the fourteen preservice teachers in our program managed to use technology to transform the science curriculum despite issues of access, compatibility, and inertia. Although our students were novices who were working with mentor teachers with little to no experience with instructional technology, and were confronted with technology-deficient situations, we discovered that they all used technology, and six of the fourteen went on to be innovators, catalyzing change and creating new instructional technology applications.

Beside the direct effects of the student teachers using instructional technology in their own teaching, there was an apparent impact on their mentor teachers. In ten of the fourteen cases, mentor teachers reported changes in how they used technology in their classroom practice. The impact ranged from considering more creative uses of existing instructional technology to purchasing new technologies (e.g., electronic microscopes and software) to revising entire curricula to take advantage of technologies the student teachers had employed.

We have yet to determine the success of our approach to technology integration in science methods courses beyond student teaching. However, the preliminary findings discussed here are promising and indicate that the impact of individual teachers who use technology can be felt beyond their classrooms. The success of a single technology-innovative teacher has the potential to influence the practices of other open-minded and committed teachers in the school. Ten of fourteen mentor teachers' views on instructional technology use have expanded as a result of their interaction with our student teachers. Whether this interaction has a lasting influence on the mentor teachers' practices, only time will tell. However, this is a hopeful beginning grounded in the realities of the classroom.

NOTE

1. WebQuests are structured inquiry-based Web activities that involve students in problem solving and role-playing. This role-playing is intended to engage the higher order thinking skills of the students. For more information, see http://edweb.sdsu.edu/webquest/webquest.html (accessed 4 January 2002).

REFERENCES

Cuban, Larry. (2001). *Oversold and underused: Computers in the classroom.* Cambridge, MA: Harvard University Press.

Fisher, Becky, Assistant Director of Technology, Albemarle County Schools. (2002, January 29). Personal communication.

Fulton, Kathleen. (2001, December). Personal communication.

3

THE IMPACT OF TECHNOLOGY ON RURAL SCHOOLS WITH STATE LEADERSHIP

James E. Eschenmann

Harrison County Board of Education, West Virginia

INTRODUCTION

This chapter shows how Harrison County—a rural county school system with limited funding—has made a difference in the lives of students by preparing them to use technology. Under our program, students are learning important skills that will help them succeed in college and in a technology-based work force.

When implementing our technology program we found that comprehensive planning and training were crucial to success. We also found that technology must be equitably distributed throughout the school system to ensure that students are exposed to technology from the time they enter kindergarten until they graduate from high school.

The implementation of technology has been a key part of education in Harrison County over the past fifteen years. We have made a concentrated effort to provide access to all students regardless of the economic or social status of their school's community. We have also tried to provide access for students who are physically or visually challenged. As of this writing, the board of education has completed a five-year plan to install new computers in every public school in the county.

Technology in Harrison County has made a significant difference in the academic lives of our students. Although our county is very economically diverse, we have eliminated the "technology divide" for our students within our schools. With all schools having computer labs and computers in the library or media center and in the majority of classrooms, students have multiple opportunities during the school day to access technology. We continue to provide multiple training opportunities for teachers, not only in the use of applications but also in the integration of these applications within the individual classroom and curriculum setting. Although computer use and integration have been customized to the local school needs, students have access to technology throughout the curriculum. We have found technology to be a great leveler of abilities and a stimulus for higher achievement.

BACKGROUND

The Harrison County School District is located in the north central portion of West Virginia. The district serves about 11,500 students in fourteen elementary, six middle, and five high schools. The district also runs two alternative/transitional schools and participates in a multicounty vocational school.

Close to 23 percent of the population of Harrison County is under the age of eighteen, a drop of roughly 24 percent since 1980. Over the same period, the number of children living in poverty has increased by almost 38 percent. Over the last twenty years, the total pupil enrollment in Harrison County Schools fell about 20 percent, whereas the total population in the county fell about 9 percent. During that same period, there was about a 17 percent drop in the number of high-paying jobs and about a 36 percent rise in the number of low-paying jobs. This shift from high- to low-paying jobs is due in part to a reduction in coal-mining activity and glass production and a corresponding increase in the number of service jobs. During this transition, the overall unemployment rate has remained stable at about 8.6 percent, although median family income, measured in 1990 dollars, declined by 1.3 percent between 1980 and 1990.

The U.S. Department of Labor predicts that information technology jobs will be among the fastest growing occupations over the next five years, and these jobs are beginning to appear in the Harrison County area. Over the last several years, the Federal Bureau of Investigation CJIS Division, Bombardier, and Northrop/Grumman have moved into the county, which have brought many new families into the area. However, the expected increase in student population has not materialized.

DEVELOPING A TECHNOLOGY PLAN

The fact that many young people were leaving Harrison County in search of better-paying jobs convinced the board of education that the county needed better training and employment opportunities, particularly in the area of technology. In the fall of 1995, a broad-based committee of administrators, teachers, service personnel, and parents was given the task of developing a comprehensive technology plan. As a first step, the committee worked with IBM and the West Virginia High Technology Consortium to develop a survey instrument that would determine the technology needs within the county. After carefully evaluating the results of the survey, the committee put together a plan that was quickly adopted by the board of education. Implementation began in the fall of 1996. The main goal of the plan was to ensure the equitable distribution of technology resources and to give every school in the county access to technology and training. By the fall of 2001, the plan had been rewritten and expanded twice. We have found that, given changing needs and continual advances in technology, it is essential to revise the plan on a regular basis.

PUTTING THE PLAN INTO EFFECT

Funding for technology in Harrison County comes from three primary sources: state-funded programs, grants, and a local excess levy. The state legislature provides funding for three programs: the Basic Skills/Computer Education program, the SUCCESS (Student Utilization of Computers in Curriculum for the Enhancement of Scholastic Skills) program, and the Telecommunications program. Additional projects are funded through technology grants and the $1.2 million per year that is raised through the local excess levy. We give a brief overview of these programs below to show how each contributed to the success of the county's technology plan.

The Basic Skills Program

In 1991, the West Virginia legislature established the Basic Skills program. This five-year program was designed to provide computers, software, and hardware that would improve basic skills learning for students in grades K–6. IBM and Jostens Learning were to provide the hardware and software. Initial implementation started at the kindergarten level. The hardware originally provided for 10-base-2 networked diskless workstations and a file server. Printers were provided as needed. These initial installations were expanded until all K–6 grade classrooms had received the hardware and software.

Training was provided for all teachers who would be participating in the program. Unfortunately, some of the training was provided long before the equipment was installed, and teachers either lost their initial enthusiasm or had to be retrained. Over the succeeding years, a great effort has been made to offer new and better training opportunities and to provide them at the proper time. This effort has paid off; we have seen a large increase in the number of teachers who are now comfortable using technology in the classroom.

This program is now in its eleventh year, and its highly successful results have been documented and verified by an outside agency. The results of this study are available from the West Virginia Department of Education Office of Technology (Mann et al., 1999).

Initially, the computers were installed only in the classroom, but more recently schools have been able to choose the type of installation that best meets the needs of their students. Some schools continue to request distributed classroom installations, others choose a lab setting that allows each class to rotate through on a scheduled basis, and still others choose a combination of the two.

The SUCCESS Program

The legislature authorized the SUCCESS initiative in 1996. This program paired Compaq Computers with various software vendors through Pomeroy Computer Resources, to provide hardware and software to grades 7–12. SUCCESS emphasizes the use of productivity tools such as Microsoft Office in the core curriculum areas, along with guidance and career exploration software such as Bridges, NewsBank, and SIGI. The program was divided into two tiers, with Tier I being the installation of network infrastructures, servers, computers, and productivity software. Tier II was the installation of the guidance and career exploration software. Even though Harrison County was allotted more than $340,000 per year, it took five years to reach full implementation of Tier I, with approximately $150,000 being spent per school. We were able to complete Tier I and implement all of Tier II in year five.

As in the Basic Skills program, schools were able to choose the type of implementation that best suited the needs of their students. Again, some chose a distributed implementation, others chose labs, and still others chose a combination of the two.

After evaluating the Basic Skills program, the West Virginia Department of Education saw that it needed to take a different approach to training. With the SUCCESS program, counties and schools were able to choose from many different training options. These options included basic training in Windows navigation, how to use Microsoft Office, integration of Microsoft Office into the core curriculum classrooms, and network administration. Program-specific training, train-the-trainer classes, and customized training designed and developed by end users and professional trainers were offered as well. Money for training was set aside, and training was scheduled to start immediately after the hardware and software had been installed. This approach has had mixed results. The various training opportunities have been successful in equipping teachers for implementation within their classrooms, but training has not been provided as quickly as had been hoped. Reasons for the delay include installation delays, weather-related problems, schedule conflicts between trainers and individual schools, and lack of time for training entire faculties. Overall, however, the training provided through the SUCCESS program has been much improved over the original training provided through the Basic Skills program.

The Telecommunications Program

The legislature authorized the Telecommunications program about seven years ago. The main goal of this program is to help ensure that all schools have equal access to the Internet. Each year under this program, Harrison County has received as few as twenty-seven computers and as many as ninety-seven. The county has distributed these computers to the schools with either the lowest number of computers or the highest student-to-computer ratios, and, as a result, they have been placed primarily in the elementary and middle schools. As with the other two state programs, schools are given the opportunity to determine whether the computers would be distributed in individual classrooms or in computer labs.

The original intent was to use these computers to improve Internet connectivity, but the computers were supplied with Microsoft Office so that they could be used to increase student and teacher productivity as well. Some schools have also used these computers in conjunction with the Compass software provided through the Basic Skills program.

The Basic Skills and SUCCESS programs provided the networking connectivity required for the installation of the computers supplied by each individual program. With the Telecommunications program, each individual school or county is responsible for the installation of required network infrastructure. This connectivity, along with electrical needs, has been provided through local excess levy funds and is in keeping with the standards and long-range goals of the county.

GRANTS

Grants from various sources have provided funding for additional programs. These grants have primarily been funded through the Technology Literacy Challenge Fund (TLCF) and the West Virginia Department of Education.

Harrison County has received three TLCF grants. The first provided money to establish a centralized training facility located in the central office. This facility is used throughout the year to train teachers and service personnel to use technology and integrate it into all aspects of their jobs. Classes range from beginning to advanced level training on Windows, Microsoft Office, and network administration, to the training of secretaries in the use of special software to produce a variety of financial reports. In addition, Marshall University, Salem International University, and West Virginia University use the lab to provide graduate-level and distance learning classes for teachers, not only from Harrison County but from the region and state as well.

The second TLCF grant provided funds to establish and equip local Cisco Academies in all Harrison County high schools and within several schools and vocational centers throughout the region. In addition, a regional Cisco Academy was established at Robert C. Byrd High School to provide instructor-level training and support for the local academies throughout the region.

The third TLCF grant provided for the installation and standardization of library automation software and hardware for all Harrison County schools. Eventually, this system will allow each school library to share its resources with every other school library in the county.

The final major technology grant received was a Multimedia Demonstration grant to enable Bridgeport Middle School to establish a multimedia/research lab. This grant provided money to purchase and install a fifteen-station computer lab with specialized software for multimedia production. We discuss this highly successful program later in this chapter.

THE LOCAL EXCESS LEVY

A local excess levy provides most of the funding for technology within Harrison County. This levy, which has been in place since 1955, now provides $1.2 million per year for technology. These funds are used to provide hardware, software, networking infrastructure, Internet connectivity, maintenance, repair, and training for all schools in the county. Five years ago, when the county's technology plan was put in place, the levy was modified to provide money for technology. A county technology committee was created to oversee the implementation of the plan, the primary goal of which was to address the equity issue among all Harrison County schools. After all the schools had been visited and inventoried, the committee developed a five-year plan to install new computers and networks in the schools. This plan was completed in 2000. As of this writing, these funds are being used to continue to upgrade computers, software, network infrastructure, and training.

A countywide network is being designed and implemented with a three- to five-year implementation plan. This network is designed to improve the quality and reliability of technology resources available to students and teachers. The plan has three major goals: (1) to consolidate servers to a centralized location to reduce the workload on building-level administrators and to ensure reliable backups and student security; (2) to converge all voice, video, and data traffic to an IP format to reduce costs and to expand offerings; and (3) to provide distance learning and virtual classes to students through an IP video network and the Internet to provide additional and advanced course offerings.

At present, Harrison County is offering one online class that was developed in-house. Called Health Online, this class is being offered to more than thirty students. Two additional classes are provided through arrangements with the Virtual School Project of the West Virginia Department of Education. Although it is still too early to formally evaluate these courses, feedback from students and teachers has been positive.

All of these new programs, taken together, have resulted in improved achievement, increased learning opportunities, and an increase in students' desire to learn.

IMPLEMENTATION OF THE TECHNOLOGY PLAN

In this section, we examine how the technology plan has been implemented in two Harrison County schools, Big Elm Elementary and Bridgeport Middle School.

Big Elm Elementary

Located in Shinnston, West Virginia, Big Elm Elementary is a pre-K–6 school that serves 692 students with two administrators and a staff of fifty. The main industry in this primarily blue-collar community is coal mining. Big Elm is a Title I school that serves free or reduced-cost lunches to 66 percent of its students. The school's one computer lab has twenty-six computers, and each individual classroom has three computers. The building is networked and is serviced by a Windows NT 4.0 server and a T-1 line. Big Elm is scheduled to receive an additional twenty-eight computers during the next school year. In addition, the network infrastructure will be upgraded to a 100Mb switched environment with a 1000Mb fiber backbone.

The use of technology at Big Elm is an integral part of its Unified School Improvement Plan. Teachers use software applications in the computer lab to assess the reading and math skills of all their students. The analyses of these results are used to individualize CE/BS (Compass) lessons so that each student is working in his or her indicated areas of need. The classroom teachers also analyze overall grade-level and classroom scores and use the results to realign the curriculum to emphasize the areas of needed improvement. As shown in table 3.1, these procedures, along with other schoolwide programs, have resulted in an increase in Stanford Achievement Test, Ninth Edition (SAT-9) scores in recent years.

The Computer Club, which meets in the computer lab in the evening or on weekends throughout the school year, is sponsored by the School-Wide Title I Committee. This club encourages parents and students to work together using technology in an educational setting. The main goal is to provide parents and students with hands-on experience that will allow them to explore the vast variety of technology that is available. In addition, Microsoft Office and the other programs and activities listed are used to enhance and augment the student's technology learning environment. These additional programs are:

- Basic Skills/Computer Education—Compass and Tomorrow's Promise
- Integrated Language Arts—Will soon be available buildingwide
- Kids Club—An extended-day program for grades 1–5 that meets after school and focuses on language arts, math, and computer skills
- Lightspan Take-Home Technology—Sony PlayStations and Lightspan educational software provided for take-home use
- Lightspan Network—Web-based education software resource for students and parents
- Morning Lightspan Club—A three-day-per-week program for at-risk students offered by Title I
- STAR Reading—Enables teachers to assess individual reading levels

Table 3.1. SAT-9 Percentile Scores (1997–2000); CTBS Percentile Scores (1992–1996)

Third Grade

	Reading			Math			
Year	Comp	Vocab.	Total	Prob.	Process	Total	Basic Skills
2000	59	56	58	73	64	68	62
1999	58	61	60	79	61	70	64
1998	63	58	61	80	68	75	67
1997	43	48	44	58	61	59	52
1996	53	61	56	80	70	76	67
1995		52				73	62
1994		61				68	61
1993		59				65	60
1992		49				58	50

Fourth Grade

	Reading			Math			
Year	Comp	Vocab.	Total	Prob.	Process	Total	Basic Skills
2000	59	59	59	64	51	58	58
1999	59	60	61	69	50	60	61
1998	47	49	47	63	50	57	52
1997	50	49	51	50	51	50	51
1996	44	37	41	38	51	45	45

Fifth Grade

	Reading			Math			
Year	Comp	Vocab.	Total	Prob.	Process	Total	Basic Skills
2000	58	61	59	66	69	68	63
1999	49	55	53	64	57	62	57
1998	63	59	62	67	68	67	63
1997	50	46	49	57	60	58	53
1996	51	45	48	58	62	61	59

Bridgeport Middle School

Bridgeport Middle School is a 6–8 school located in Bridgeport, West Virginia; it serves 634 students with two administrators and a staff of forty. Bridgeport is not a Title I school. The community it serves is primarily white collar; the free or reduced lunch rate is 22 percent. Constructed in 1995, the building was designed with three twenty-four-station computer labs; a computerized tech education lab was installed in 1996. In addition, each classroom was wired for five workstations, although not all drops had computers attached. Over the last several years, two additional computer labs and many classroom workstations have been added using Basic Skills, SUCCESS, and grant funding. The building is networked through a 100Mb switched environment with a 1000Mb fiber backbone, a Windows NT 4.0 server, and two T-1 lines. The building network is currently being expanded to connect to Bridgeport High School, which is located adjacent to Bridgeport Middle School. Plans are in place to add Johnson Elementary—located next to the high school—to the network as well. Eventually, all three schools will be part of one large network. This will improve security; facilitate administration and the sharing of resources; and provide faster, more reliable Internet service.

The three of the computer labs are available for core curriculum teachers to use with an entire class. These labs are used continually and are scheduled by sign-up. They provide Internet access for research, productivity tools, and Basic Skills software. Teachers can use resources in the labs to assess student performance, diagnose individual needs, and provide remediation and accelerated activities.

The two remaining labs are used for scheduled computer classes. Most of the students rotate through these labs twice a year for a six-week class. One lab is used to teach basic productivity skills using Microsoft Office and Internet navigation skills. Under this program, students expand and reinforce their skills each year. The other lab is used for research and multimedia activities. The equipment and software in this lab were provided by a multimedia demonstration grant from the West Virginia Department of Education.

The research and multimedia lab is equipped with fifteen Windows NT 4.0 workstations equipped with Microsoft Office. All computers are networked into the building local area network (LAN) and have Internet connectivity. The lab is located in a classroom that is directly beside, and connected to, the school media center. The building network administrator and media specialist use the lab for an engaged learning research class that is team-taught. Students are rotated through the class on a six-week basis. They are taught, and are expected to use, research and note-taking skills, both in the media center and on the Internet, and production skills using Microsoft Office 2000 applications (PowerPoint,

Word, and Publisher). The students are given specific research problems and then are expected to present their results in the form of a multimedia research project using either PowerPoint or Publisher. These can be individual or group projects. Sometimes the students of an entire class or team work on a project with the assistance of all the subject area teachers.

THE ROLE OF TECHNOLOGY IN MOTIVATING STUDENTS

Harrison County's technology program has been highly successful. It is giving our students the research skills they will need for further education and is allowing them to use and expand their creative abilities by using the multimedia components. What's more, this technology makes the traditional research paper *fun*. Students are no longer constrained to using just pencil and paper to recite dull facts. Technology has also proven to be a great leveler of ability. Slower students can participate and experience success in the same areas as the advanced students, who can now expand their abilities beyond the normal constraints of the classroom and textbook. Technology can also be used to target needs areas identified by the core curriculum teachers. The research teachers can customize projects to meet a student's specific needs while still teaching the research and multimedia skills required of the class.

We have seen students with serious discipline problems become settled students and high achievers. With this new technology, students who have never had an opportunity to use their creative abilities now have an avenue for expression. The "D" and "F" students can now achieve an "A" or "B" on the same level as the more advanced students. Technology is not a panacea for all problems, but it has made a significant difference for many students.

OPERATIONAL PROBLEMS

Despite the overall success of the technology program in Harrison County, there have been a few problems. We have analyzed these problems as they have come up and have addressed them in the best manner available to us. We have also tried to anticipate and prevent future problems.

A major problem is service. As technology evolves, operating systems and networks become more complicated, machines break, files become corrupted, and older machines will not work with newer software. We now have a service contract with a local systems integration company to provide service and parts for most of our machines, all file servers, and all network resources. This arrangement has worked extremely well. Computer downtime has been reduced while network reliability and performance have both improved. Harrison County has a large number of pre-Pentium computers that are still in use. The cost to replace all of these machines would be prohibitive at this point, but we are starting to install terminal servers in the schools that have these older machines. We can service 400 older computers with one $30,000 terminal server as opposed to spending over $500,000 to replace them. This still provides schools with the latest software and productivity tools needed for classroom work and will allow for a longer replacement schedule.

Another problem has been teachers who do not want to participate in computer training and do not want to use technology in their classrooms. We have greatly increased the number and availability of technology-related courses offered at individual schools and countywide. We now have trainers available in all of our middle and high schools who can teach others to use the software provided through the SUCCESS program. The Basic Skills program has funded a part-time consultant for the elementary and middle schools. Money is also available for substitutes and outside instructors, thus allowing teachers to attend training sessions in our technology learning center during the workday without having to leave the building. As more teachers become excited about technology and all that it can accomplish, the resistant teachers are beginning to wake up and get on board. It is primarily the older teachers nearing retirement who don't want to use technology, but as state and local requirements expand to make technology a component in every subject area, these teachers, too, are becoming more receptive to the use of technology.

CONCLUSION

The successful use of computers in Harrison County Schools can be attributed to the Basic Skills/Computer Education and SUCCESS programs, along with the willingness of the Harrison County Board of Education and the people of Harrison County to put into place an excess
levy that has provided additional funding for technology. Comprehensive planning is the most crucial component of technology implementation. School systems must look at the overall implementation and distribution of technology, not just in a single school but in the district as a
whole. Standardization and training, along with service and maintenance, must also be considered. Without any one of these components,
the implementation will fail. Each of these elements is costly, but all are
necessary to ensure that students and teachers are not disillusioned and
frustrated because the equipment doesn't work or because they don't
know how to use it.

Computers and technology will never replace the classroom teacher,
and they are not a cure for all the problems in education. They are, however, exciting tools that have almost unlimited possibilities for educational use. It will take time for the best practices to come to light and for
the best software to be sorted out and deployed. In Harrison County, we
believe that technology is an indispensable tool for education if we are
to give our students the best possible education and prepare them for
the real world they will face.

REFERENCE

Mann, Dale, Shakeshaft, Charol, Becker, Jonathan, & Kottkamp, Robert.
   (1999). *West Virginia story: Achievement gains from a statewide comprehensive instructional technology program.* New York: Columbia University.

4

BUILDING A COMMUNITY OF LIFELONG LEARNERS

Christine Richards
Doddridge County Schools, West Virginia

Ten years ago, while visiting a neighboring school, I had the opportunity to view an exciting new worldwide database called the Internet. The Doddridge County school system has embraced this new teaching and learning paradigm and focuses on how technology can augment educational reforms to achieve our educational objectives.

BACKGROUND

The Doddridge County School District is located in the north central part of West Virginia. The district serves roughly 1,250 students in four elementary schools, one middle school, and one high school. The four elementary schools were consolidated into a single new school that opened in August 2002. The district also has an alternative program for middle and high school students, and it participates in a multicounty vocational school as well.

Doddridge is a small rural county that has no major industry; the state and local governments are the county's two largest employers. The county has a population of about 7,400 and a per capita personal income (PCPI) of $15,764. Roughly 30 percent of the children live in poverty (U.S. Census Bureau, 2000).

Fifty-two percent of our students receive free or reduced-cost meals. Four of our six schools qualify for Title I services, and about 200 students (16 percent) participate in the program. Title I is a federally funded program designed to assist students who are having difficulty with math or reading skills.

Doddridge County residents have long provided strong support to their local school system even when it has meant financial hardship. This support was evident when the residents passed the school levy, which has been a critical funding source for implementing school reform. Results of a countywide survey completed by the Doddridge County Family Resource Network (FRN) show that residents believe education to be an important investment for the county's future. The success or failure of school reforms relies heavily on parent and community support and commitment (NCREL, 1999).

THE IMPACT OF STATEWIDE TECHNOLOGY INITIATIVES

In recent years, there has been a major paradigm shift in education from theories of learning to theories of cognition. Rather than focusing on teaching facts through lectures or demonstrations, the emphasis is instead on developing higher-order thinking and problem-solving skills. Teachers are being asked to learn new instructional approaches so that students can meet tough new learning standards (NCREL, 1999).

Educational technology has played an important role in Doddridge County as teachers embrace the shift with education reform. Statewide initiatives and policies have directly influenced the shift from traditional teacher-directed learning to a student-engaged learning built on the integration of higher-order thinking skills.

Statewide technology initiatives have paved the way for educational reform in Doddridge County. The first such turnkey program, West Virginia's Basic Skill/Computer Education (BS/CE) program, provided all of our K–6 classrooms with computers, software programs, and training. The Basic Skills program was initiated in 1990 and funded by the West Virginia Legislature. It is considered the nation's most comprehensive statewide approach to computer education (WVDE, 1999).

The project was implemented in the kindergarten and first grade and has been integrated through the sixth grade. Our county uses both the Jostens Learning System in Reading and Mathematics and the IBM Basic Skills Courseware programs. Both software programs are aligned with the national standards and our state's instructional goals and objectives (IGOs) and targets. The programs target IGOs that needed improvement in mathematics, reading, and language arts.

Although both the Jostens and IBM programs are aligned with national and state standards, they differ in their approach to instructional practices. Both programs allow for individualized student-based instruction; however, the IBM program promotes small group activities and cooperative learning that lead toward individual independent work. The IBM solution promotes problem solving and higher-order thinking skills, whereas the Jostens solution promotes critical thinking skills.

The Milken Family Foundation commissioned Interactive, Inc., of New York to conduct an independent study that analyzed student achievement in the West Virginia BS/CE program. The study was conducted by Professor Dale Mann of the Teachers College at Columbia University; Professor Charol Shakeshaft of Hofstra University; Jonathan Becker, J.D., a research specialist in law and education at Columbia University; and Dr. Robert Kottkamp, a professor in the Department of Administration and Policy Studies at Hofstra University (Mann, 1999).

The results of the study showed that "BS/CE worked" (Mann, 1999). "Mann, Shakeshaft, Becker, and Kottkamp conclude that the 11 percent of the total variance in the basic skills achievement gain scores (from 1995–1996 to 1996–1997) can be explained by participation in BS/CE" (Mann, 1999). The study also provided reasons why the BS/CE program was effective in improving student achievement (Mann, 1999):

- Rather than isolating computer skills from academic learning, West Virginia's BS/CE program integrated technology into the instructional program. In other words, the technology was a means of learning the basics, not an end in itself.
- The report revealed that the computers inside classrooms were more effective than centralized computer labs in producing basic skill gains in students and in promoting the confidence and technological competence of teachers.

• The report also revealed the importance of timely and comprehensive teacher training as a key factor in the success of West Virginia's technology program (West Virginia Study Results).

In 1996, West Virginia was one of two states, according to National Assessment of Educational Progress (NAEP), to see improved math scores in three categories (WVDE, 1999). In a 1999–2000 executive summary, the West Virginia Department of Education's Office of Student Services and Assessment stated that between 1996 and 2000, fourth grade students had significantly improved their scores on the Stanford Achievement Test, Ninth Edition (SAT-9).

For Doddridge County's fourth graders, the mean percentile SAT scores for Total Basic Skills rose from the 52nd percentile in 1996–1997 to the 60th percentile in 1999–2000; statewide, fourth graders' scores increased from the 58th to the 64th percentile. The scores of fifth and sixth grade students also increased, both in Doddridge County and in the state as a whole. Table 4.1 lists these scores.

The success of the BS/CE program in Doddridge County is directly linked to the turnkey solution provided under the West Virginia legislation. Former West Virginia State Superintendent Dr. Henry Marockie stated that, "The turnkey solution, which coupled intensive professional development with installation of standardized hardware and software make this program succeed" (WVDE, 1999). He also stated: "Teachers embraced the technology because they were able to acquire the background, knowledge, and expertise to make it happen" (WVDE, 1999).

Table 4.1. Mean Percentile (SAT) Scores for Total Basic Skills, Statewide and in Doddridge County

Doddridge	1996–1997	1997–1998	1998–1999	1999–2000
4th	52	59	64	60
5th	44	50	57	64
6th	59	57	60	71
Statewide	1996–1997	1997–1998	1998–1999	1999–2000
4th	58	61	62	64
5th	28	60	62	63
6th	63	65	65	66

The BS/CE program worked in Doddridge County because all of the stakeholders bought into the program, from the governor and the legislature to teachers and parents.

Doddridge County is in the process of migrating from the Jostens Learning System in Reading and Mathematics and the IBM Basic Skills Courseware to a CompassLearning curriculum solution. What induced our teachers to integrate CompassLearning into the curriculum was the C-Pass component. C-Pass evaluates student performances on the objectives stated in national standards and West Virginia's IGOs. After evaluating a student's academic strengths and weaknesses, C-Pass prescribes appropriate lessons from the CompassLearning curriculum for individualized learning paths. Teachers are given immediate feedback on students' results and progress.

The new Doddridge County Elementary School, which opened in the fall of 2002, is adopting the CompassLearning program. The elementary technology team and the county technology coordinator have established procedures for implementing schoolwide use of CompassLearning.

The school will have a computer lab with twenty-five Internet, multimedia, networked workstations and the capacity to add five more. All teachers will have a scheduled time during the week in which their students can use the lab.

In addition to the computer lab, each classroom will have access to the CompassLearning program. Each will have a minimum of three Internet, multimedia, networked workstations capable of accessing CompassLearning and the capacity to add six more.

The West Virginia State Board of Education has adopted a new content-based policy to replace the current IGOs. Policy 2520, Content Standards and Objectives for West Virginia Schools, emphasizes incorporated content based on the most current research, national standards, and best teaching practices in the field (WVDE). Each content area begins with a set of content standards. Grade-level objectives are then organized under the standards, so that the focus stays on helping students achieve the comprehensive goals, not just mastering the incremental steps.

With this new state-level education reform, CompassLearning has made a commitment to align the new standards with the existing software solution, thereby providing teachers with the same capability to assess students and individualize learning based on academic needs.

Following the success of the BS/CE program, West Virginia launched a second statewide technology initiative, which has had a significant impact on education reform in Doddridge County. The West Virginia SUCCESS (Student Utilization of Computers in Curriculum for the Enhancement of Scholastic Skills) initiative provides technology to prepare students for the workplace and for postsecondary education. All counties were allowed to decide how the program would be implemented within their local school systems.

Doddridge County's technology team, which was led by the county superintendent and included seventh- through twelfth-grade teachers and the technology coordinator, decided to begin by placing three Internet, multimedia networked computers in each seventh- and eighth-grade classroom and installing a computer lab in the high school that would be accessible to all teachers.

The continued support of the state legislature has made it possible for both the middle school and the high school to have access to an open computer lab. Each of the seventh- and eighth-grade classrooms now has five Internet, multimedia networked computers, and each of the ninth- through twelfth-grade classrooms has three.

With the SUCCESS program's emphasis on preparing students for either the work force or postsecondary education, Doddridge County has expanded course offerings that develop technology and informational literacy skills. The curriculum changes were based on ISTE (International Society for Technology in Education) technology standards for students, which address the employment needs of our area and have been adopted by the state department of education.

The business community, according to the Department of Labor report *What Work Requires of Students*, identifies five required skills: resource allocation skills, interpersonal skills, information skills, systems skills, and technology skills. These skills are required in the expanding global economy in which American business must operate (WVBEA, 1995). The West Virginia Schools-to-Work initiative will help students to connect school and life after school and will motivate students to take greater interest in their education. To achieve this reform, Doddridge County High School changed its curriculum offerings to include more computer, technology, and business courses.

Before our curriculum and technology team developed the new technology courses, local businesses were surveyed by phone and asked what technology-related skills were essential for employment. The committee also worked with the DeVry Institute's curriculum development department to develop curriculum outlines that would prepare students who choose to attend postsecondary training.

Ten years ago, keyboarding was an elective course and was taught using electric typewriters. Typically, only college-bound students or students who planned a career in a secretarial field (mostly females) opted to take the keyboard course. Today, keyboarding is a required course and is taught with computer literacy based on state and ISTE standards. All students graduate with basic computer literacy skills.

Because they have been learning keyboarding skills from kindergarten through eighth grade, many ninth-grade students test out of the required keyboarding/computer literacy programs and are able to choose a higher-level technology-related course. Doddridge County High School offers the following technology-related courses that either prepare students directly for the job market or serve as prerequisites for postsecondary education: Advance Business Computer Application, including word processing (Microsoft Word), spreadsheet (Excel), database (Access), and PowerPoint (prepares students for the MOUS certification); C++ Programming; Oracle Data Base Programming (prepares students for Oracle certification); and desktop publishing.

Doddridge County High School was selected as one of only seven schools in the state of West Virginia to participate in the Oracle Internet Academy pilot program sponsored by the Oracle Corporation. This cutting-edge curriculum provides students with training in database fundamentals, database programming (SQL), Java programming, and Java database applications. West Virginia has developed and adopted curriculum standards based on the Oracle program.

Currently, we have fifteen students in database fundamentals, which is the first in a series of four courses. Thirteen students will continue on to the second course, database programming (SQL). Students also have the option to attend a tri-county technical school for training in information systems and the Cisco Academy (to prepare for Cisco certification). The technical school provides our students with a free fifth year of schooling to complete necessary training for certifications after high school graduation.

Students are far more computer savvy than they were even five years ago. Why? These same students began their technology travels under the West Virginia BS/CE program in kindergarten more than ten years ago. Curriculum needs drive what technology is purchased. We do not obtain technology for the sake of having technology.

IMPACT OF THE INTERNET

The third statewide technology initiative that influenced education reform in Doddridge County was developed in 1994 through a partnership between Bell Atlantic-West Virginia (Verizon) and the West Virginia State Department of Education. This partnership provided free access to the Internet to all West Virginia schools through the West Virginia Network for Educational Telecomputing (WVNET) server. Doddridge County was the eleventh school in the state to connect to the Internet via direct frame relay technology.

Parker J. Palmer, a well-known speaker and educator, states:

> To sit in a class where the teacher stuffs our minds with information, organizes it with finality, insists on having the answer while being utterly uninterested in our views, and forces us into a grim competition for grades—to sit in such a class is to experience a lack of space for learning. But to study with a teacher who not only speaks but listens, who not only gives answers but asks questions and welcomes our insights, who provides information and theories that do not close doors but open new ones, who encourages student to help each other learn—to study with such a teacher is to know the power of a learning space. (NASBE, 2001)

He bases this philosophy on the story of Abba Felix and his spiritual tradition: To teach is to create a space in which obedience to truth is practiced (Palmer, 1993). The Internet is a huge enabler of this powerful, exciting, and flexible teaching initiative. It provides the students in Doddridge County with a space wherein truth can be explored. No longer do students have to sit in a classroom where they are limited to what the teacher perceives as truth and knowledge.

To remain competitive with other school systems in offering advance courses, we now provide e-learning experiences for our students at the high school level. Students can select online courses that meet the curriculum outlined by the state department of education.

Evidence to date convincingly demonstrates that, when used appropriately, electronically delivered education, "e-learning" can provide high-quality learning opportunities to all children. (NASBE, 2001)

Every classroom in Doddridge County has access to the Internet. A 1999 County Technology Needs Assessment Survey reveals some astonishing facts concerning teacher use of the Internet. On the elementary level, only 20 percent of the teachers frequently integrated Internet activities into their curriculum, 40 percent accessed the Internet rarely, and another 40 percent did not access the Internet at all. The survey shows that use of the Internet increases in middle school. Here, 40 percent of the teachers frequently integrate Internet activities into the curriculum, 17 percent rarely use the Internet, and 43 percent do not use the Internet at all. At the high school level, 53 percent of the teachers use the Internet frequently, 36 percent use it rarely, and only 11 percent do not use it at all.

The survey shows why the Internet is integrated more often at the high school level than at the middle school and elementary levels. Technology training for the K–6 program has in the past focused on the Basic Skills integrated software program, whereas training in grades 7–12 has focused on technology integration of Microsoft Office and the Internet. Teachers' attitudes regarding the use of the Internet differ depending on the type of training that has been offered to them.

IMPACT OF TRAINING AND STAFF DEVELOPMENT

Researcher Jennifer O'Day indicates that teachers' attitudes toward change, commitment to student learning, and views of their own abilities all affect their capacity to help students meet tough standards (O'Day, 1996). When the teacher is a lifelong learner, students are the beneficiaries. Doddridge County's greatest obstacle with education reform is changing teacher attitudes toward the true meaning of technology integration.

With this issue in mind, Doddridge County initiated a county education reform project called Partnerships on the Right TRACK (Technology Resources Accessibility Collaboration Knowledge). Funding was provided through the Technology Literacy Challenge Fund. The project promotes education reform to increase student achievement and integrate technology into the classroom. The aim of the TRACK program is to

- Change teacher attitudes toward technology;
- Infuse classrooms with an exemplary model of technology use in which students acquire curriculum knowledge;
- Create self-reliant technical and application experts within each school who can support teachers and students as they integrate technology into content; and
- Through the turnkey solution, allow teachers to develop outstanding technology programs that will ensure that students achieve at higher levels and become more active, confident, and motivated learners.

Staff development is the key element of the TRACK program's success. The train-the-trainer approach was used based on the states' Technology Standards for Teachers Policy 5100. TRACK participants received hardware and software for their classrooms and training that provided a clearer understanding of the capabilities and potential of technology-integration strategies. Participants were required not only to use technology in their own classrooms but also to train other teachers at their respective schools based on local needs.

According to a post technology survey of TRACK participants, teachers improved their skills in several areas of computer literacy and developed new teaching techniques involving the integration of technology within the curriculum. Following are some of the teachers' comments regarding the training:

- "This class has challenged me to pursue other computer courses."
- "Technology provides students with an interesting way of learning, and teachers with new and exciting methods of teaching. I'm excited about the direction of education and the part technology is playing in the outcome."

- "I feel more confident about using this technology in my classroom. I intend to use PowerPoint presentations in my classroom with various themes."
- "I learned more ways to integrate technology into my classroom and lesson plans." "I feel quite comfortable with this program (PowerPoint) and will make use of its features for classroom presentations and remediation."
- "Courses such as this empower and enable those employed in education."
- "My professional development goal for the year has been to become more knowledgeable in technology and to be able to integrate technology in my classroom. I believe now that I am on my way to accomplishing my goal."
- "The integration of technology into the current curriculum now appears to be a great help in the delivery of services rather than a hindrance."

This program has provided the Doddridge County school system with educators who can function as classroom innovators and assume the leadership role in helping to implement successful models and approaches for the use of educational technology.

For the Doddridge County school system, technology has played a vital role in education reform. We have witnessed a change in the way technology is used. Ten years ago, when I would ask a student sitting at a computer what he was doing, he was likely to reply, "I am working on the computer." Today, that student would be likely to say, "I am working on my spelling lesson." This illustrates the positive pedagogical shift of seamless infusion in technology use within the school curriculum.

With the advances in technology, we must ensure that our students become technologically literate (NCREL, 1999). Doddridge County educators have realized the potential of technology use within the curriculum, not mistaking technology for a means to an end but rather seeing it as a way of enhancing relative learning experiences. Technology is a tool just as a pencil is a tool. Its only limitation is the person using it.

For students and educators in Doddridge County, technology has changed the way we learn and teach. Students and teachers perceive technology as an avenue that engages the learner in exploration and discovery of true knowledge.

What we are experiencing with the wave of technology integration in Doddridge County is best expressed by Robert Tinker: "We are helping write the script of the opening scenes of the most dramatic play educators have ever witnessed. Our grandchildren will write the final scene, and their children will enjoy its impact" (NASBE, 2001).

CONCLUSION

Through implementing state and local technology initiatives, I have had the privilege to witness classrooms in Doddridge County migrating from assembly-line entities to engaged classrooms in which students learn through interaction, working collaboratively, and exploring. Self-directed learners evolve into lifelong learners, which is the heart of our county's mission statement. Technology is the hook that makes the learning experience more authentic and meaningful.

All of our schools exhibit successful implementation of technology-based school reforms. Not all teachers integrate technology on a daily basis, but all are making an effort to explore new teaching methods and strategies. Training based on teacher needs has proven to increase usage and creativity with technology integration.

Hundreds of thousands of children in countries around the world are living the reality of the global village in personal, hands-on, and interactive ways. The only place where most of our students can learn and discover how to become citizens of this global village is in our schools. Doddridge County administrators, teachers, and students have proven the value of weaving technology throughout the curriculum to meet educational objectives.

REFERENCES

Mann, Dale, Shakeshaft, Charol, Becker, Jonathan, & Kottkamp, Robert. (1999). *West Virginia story: Achievement gains from a statewide comprehensive instructional technology program.* New York: Columbia University.

National Association of State Boards of Education (NASBE). (2001). *Any time, any place, any path, any pace: Taking the lead on e-learning policy*, at www.nasbe.org/e_Learning.html.

North Central Regional Education Laboratory (NCREL). (2000, November). *The implementation of the comprehensive school reform demonstration program*, at http://ncrel.org/csri/respub/dempro40/parent.htm.

North Central Regional Educational Laboratory (NCREL). (1999). *Technology connections for school improvement*, at www.ncrel.org.

O'Day, J., Fuhrman, S. (1996). *Rewards and reform: Creating educational incentives that work*. San Francisco: Jossey-Bass.

Palmer, P.J. (1993). *To know as we are known: Education as a spiritual journey*. San Francisco: Harper & Row.

United States Census Bureau. (2000). United States Department of Commerce, at www.census.gov.

West Virginia Business and Education Alliance (WVBEA). (1995). *Ready for what? What employers expect What higher education requires What students need*. Charleston, WV: WVBEA.

West Virginia Department of Education State Board Policies (n.d.), at http://wvde.state.wv.us/policies/.

The West Virginia Department of Education (WVDE). (1999). *The West Virginia technology program cited for increasing student achievement*, at http://wvde.state.wv.us/news/16/.

5

BUILDING THE BRIDGE TO
EFFECTIVE USE OF TECHNOLOGY

Blake C. West

Blue Valley Schools, Kansas

For some people, integrating technology in schools means using computers for word processing, delivering lectures with PowerPoint, building skills with drill-and-practice software, and perhaps looking up information on the Internet as if it were an encyclopedia. This description of technology use is little more than automating the school of the early twentieth century. Technology has far more to offer, but its potential is not likely to be realized without thoughtful design of curriculum, instructional practice, and strategies for implementation in the classroom. In this review, we look at how one Midwestern suburban school district fostered conditions that support and encourage teachers as they use technology to enhance student learning. We also rethink what "effective use of technology" means for both students and teachers as we consider numerous examples of effective use. Finally, we draw some conclusions about what has worked well and what hasn't, and the conditions that have contributed to success.

CONTEXT

Blue Valley USD 229 is a growing district on the Kansas side of the state line in the suburbs of Kansas City, Missouri. The Blue Valley community has a long history of support for public schools and for technology in schools. This has been evidenced by community passage of major school bond initiatives that include funding for the construction of new state-of-the-art facilities to meet growth needs and for technological upgrades of existing facilities. Although the funding system in the state of Kansas limits the per-pupil amount a school district can spend for operational expenses, school bonds for construction provide an additional means of support.

Blue Valley has done more than purchase hardware for schools. Since 1987, the district has asked classroom teachers who were technology leaders to provide professional development for their colleagues. To encourage teachers to use computers, the district initiated a series of graduate credit courses (developed and taught by district teachers under agreements with the continuing education departments of local universities). In the late 1980s and early 1990s, teachers who completed a core of thirty hours of training were "permanently" loaned either a Macintosh or a Windows-based computer that they could use in their homes or classrooms.

The professional development program grew throughout the 1990s to include a variety of credit courses and shorter workshops. At one time, the district had issued more than 900 computers to staff members who had completed their thirty hours of training. When it became known that the computer loan program might be discontinued, many staff members came to meetings to argue in favor of the program. They brought samples of the kinds of work they had been able to do with access to a machine that allowed them to work at home. Despite this evidence, the district eventually had to end the program. Confronted with a teaching force that was increasing by 50 to 100 teachers per year, the need to upgrade the equipment of the early recipients, a change in the Kansas state school-funding formula, and the fact that state funding was not keeping up with inflation, Blue Valley was forced to discontinue the computer loan program and trust that employees would buy their own computers and continue to work at home.

Even after the loan program ended, the staff-development offerings continued to be in high demand; many teachers were hooked on technology both as a productivity tool and as a teaching and learning resource. A large proportion of the staff continues to take workshops or courses every time a new offering is developed (over 95 percent have taken at least one technology course offered through the district). Feedback from participants has indicated that the strengths of the professional development program can be attributed to three factors: (1) sessions were offered at a variety of convenient times, (2) peers (district teachers) taught the sessions based on their understanding of the district curriculum and the realities of work in classrooms, and (3) the content of the sessions focused not only on skill development but also on the use of technology to support effective teaching practices.

Rather than simply assigning some arbitrary number of computers to each classroom in the district, hardware has been allocated based on the specific demands of the curriculum. Over the last few years, the district has migrated almost entirely to a Windows-based environment. (The exceptions are the journalism and art departments.) Fiber-optic networking provides high-speed Internet access in every building, classroom, and work area. Each time a curricular area undergoes a review or revision, a technology "expert" participates in the process to help identify tools that might enhance student learning and where technology can best be integrated to ensure that learning goals are met. In the last two years, curricular revisions have been placed online along with links to support materials and lesson suggestions. Specialized equipment is in place to support such programs as art, music, computer science, industrial technology (technology education), and video editing and television.

SIGNIFICANT USES OF TECHNOLOGY

With technology in place, what difference can it make in a classroom, and how can it enhance student learning? In Blue Valley, we have realized that these questions are not unlike asking how any other tool in a classroom can enhance student learning. By itself, technology does nothing. But we now know much about "best practices" for teaching, learning, and school improvement. Technology clearly supports best practices and thus can make a difference for kids and learning. In this review, examples of effective use are broken into six general areas in which technology can make a difference in teaching and learning:

- Active engagement of learners
- Building understanding through experience and exploration
- Use of real-world activities and assessments
- Meeting the needs of diverse learners
- Connecting with parents
- Professional development

Keep in mind that entire books have been written about each of these six areas. Each area is briefly covered here, but we encourage readers to do further exploration on their own.

ACTIVE ENGAGEMENT OF LEARNERS

The first group of examples deals with getting learners focused (active engagement) on the concepts to be learned. By actively engaging students in their learning, it is possible to raise the level of achievement and to increase our expectations for them (Krajewski & Parker, 2001). Students of the twenty-first century are consumers of media and expect to be entertained and engaged by their environment. Effective classrooms use instructional practices and materials that encourage students to actively participate in the learning process (Cone, 2001). For example, students are more motivated when the resource materials they use are visually interesting, involve multimedia (more than just text and still pictures), and are interactive rather than passive. Primary sources of information can be used to increase student involvement by making students into researchers as opposed to consumers of summarized, digested content. Teaching and classroom management techniques should involve a higher percentage of students in discussion and reflection on content. Following is a discussion of some of the ways that teachers in Blue Valley work to achieve these characteristics through use of technology.

Use of computers with students in early grades must be judiciously matched to appropriate learning outcomes—often, manipulative and hands-on types of experience are superior as motivators and are better matched to the concrete learning style of younger students. One example of software that is matched to curricular outcomes in an appropriate manner and that students thoroughly enjoy is Numbers Undercover (Sunburst). This program provides a variety of situations in which students learn about the values of various coins and practice making change. Another portion of the software helps students practice reading both analog and digital clocks. In addition to these practical life skills, the software works with students to develop mathematical reasoning as they analyze numeric sequences, count by numbers other than one, count backwards, etc.

Curriculum-related websites are used to draw students into the learning process. For example, Neuroscience for Kids (http://faculty.washington.edu/chudler/neurok.html) includes animations that demonstrate the operation of the nervous system. The Yuckiest Site on the Internet (www.nj.com/yucky) is popular and highly entertaining and provides good information for upper elementary and middle school science students. Middle school students also use a variety of sites with up-to-date weather information to study storms, particularly hurricanes since they can be tracked over a period of several days. At the high school, students use data from the U.S. Weather Service (isobar maps and satellite data, for example) to learn about weather forecasting. Students are much more engaged when they use "real" data than when they rely on textbooks alone as a resource. As the district curriculum has been placed online, in-service workshops have been used to make teachers aware that they have quick access to relevant and up-to-date websites that are directly linked to district and state learning outcomes.

Elementary schools in Blue Valley make use of such software as The Logical Journey of the Zoombinis (Broderbund, The Learning Company) with students in upper elementary to middle-level grades. The software presents problems that require comparing, grouping, sorting, graphing, and even algebraic thinking. We discovered that the problems were so entertaining that adults in workshops learning to teach with the software were reluctant to quit "playing" the game. The most impressive testimonial to the value of this software, though, is to observe a group of students working together to move through the "levels" of complexity. There is a tremendous synergy as students propose hypotheses about how to solve a problem, test them, analyze the results, and eventually reach a desired goal. By using computer software with students working in small cooperative groups, there is a much higher level of engagement and participation than if a similar activity is done as a whole class. Paper and pencil problem-solving activities cannot compare to the creative, interactive, and attractive graphics in a well-designed piece of software.

Math teachers have long used the machine or factory idea (a device with "input" and "output") to teach the concept of "functions." Helping students build that connection and the skill of analyzing what will happen to a given input as it passes through a machine is the task of software called The Factory Deluxe (Sunburst). In this software, geometric objects have "manipulations" performed on them by the factory. Students may either attempt to design a machine that will produce a given result, predict the results from a machine whose design is known, or try to increase the efficiency of a machine by generating the desired output in the fewest number of manipulations. This program is highly engaging, and it supports the development of reasoning skills and three-dimensional geometric visualization skills as well.

Animals in Their World (Edunetics/Sunburst) helps to address several desired learning outcomes. From the science curriculum, it allows students to explore a multimedia database of information about animals. The data can help students classify animals, learn about habitat, and begin to appreciate the food chain. Students also use the software to address language arts (communication) outcomes as they assemble video clips and pictures, and add their own text to create presentations. The rich multimedia content of the video clips and the power of allowing students to build their own presentations attracts students to the learning tasks supported by the software.

A few years ago, we began showing teachers how they could use "threaded discussion" as a tool to conduct curriculum review and materials evaluation in an online and asynchronous environment, thus saving time in meetings. Immediately, they recognized a tool they could use with their students since over 90 percent of the community has Internet access in the home. Several teachers began adding online discussions to their homework. Their reports are consistent with feedback from teachers online: Student responses are more thoughtful and complete, and all students can be engaged in discussion in a manner that is not possible in face-to-face teacher led discussions. In April 2001, a similar tool was brought into the classroom through an experimental grant program. A class of students was issued iPAQ handheld computers with wireless telecommunications capability and a dialogue software package. The teacher can now pose a question to the class and have all students respond immediately, have all responses appear on the teacher's computer screen, and send select responses (with or without attribution) to students for further discussion. Engagement of all students in a discussion not unlike that of the asynchronous discussion board occurs because the teacher is able to see the comments of every student regardless of how timid and to allow students who take a moment to think to still get in on the discussion. The combination of traditional discussion with PDA discussion also can meet the learning and interaction styles of a variety of learners in the classroom. Needless to say, the PDAs also became a resource for word processing, keeping calendars, and even playing games. This has increased productivity at times, but it has also created a need for more "supervision" schoolwide as teachers attempt to ensure that students are on task.

BUILDING UNDERSTANDING THROUGH EXPERIENCE AND EXPLORATION: CONSTRUCTIVIST LEARNING

The second tool for improved learning is to build understanding through experimentation and exploration (Marzano, Pickering, & Pollock, 2001). Using this "constructivist" approach, students build conceptual understanding through their experience in working with a problem rather than by simply having concepts presented to them (Applefield, Huber, & Moallem, 2000/2001). Many opportunities are available for students to explore, test hypotheses, verify the validity of concepts, etc., through the use of technology. Blue Valley has a long history of using a constructivist approach to help students build their understanding of algebraic concepts through the use of graphing calculator technology. Students use the devices to examine how various parameters affect the behavior of functions. They generate and test hypotheses, then follow up their experiments with writing assignments that allow them to synthesize and reflect on what was learned. More recently, graphing technology and computer software (with programs such as Geometer's Sketchpad and Cabri) have been used to allow students to do similar hypothesis testing of geometric principles. In addition to building conceptual understanding, students follow up by using logical reasoning and proof to "build" a mathematical system.

In one school, fifth-grade students had become quite proficient in the use of HyperStudio multimedia presentations. These presentations represented a culmination of their research on a variety of topics. The research work included learning outcomes related to information literacy: effective search strategies and judging the relevance of information and quality of sources, for example. The students were responsible for synthesizing information from a variety of sources in their research.

This project went a step further when the fifth graders became teachers/mentors for second- and third-grade students who were working on presentations as part of their government unit. Students in the fifth grade benefited from the experience of teaching the younger students. They internalized the skills needed to use HyperStudio as well as the skills needed to produce effective presentations. When the project was demonstrated at districtwide technology visits in April 2001, people from other elementary schools expressed an interest in developing similar peer teaching projects.

One of the most exciting places for a constructivist approach to teaching and learning is in social studies. Teachers have begun to use primary sources, such as the eyewitness accounts of participants in the Civil War, to allow students to become historians and researchers (Shawhan, 1998). Online databases of primary source information give students the opportunity to understand perspective, gain empathy, and even view events of the modern world with a more mature, reflective eye. Further, students can discuss and debate the issues and create projects such as newsletters of the time period. A final touch of relevance is added by drawing analogies with internal conflicts that are occurring today in countries such as Kosovo, Afghanistan, and Somalia.

USE OF REAL-WORLD ACTIVITIES AND ASSESSMENTS

Assignments and assessments that arise out of real-world problem (authentic learning) situations have "face validity" and seem to result in greater student learning. This might be because there is a natural "active engagement" of students when they believe that their work is relevant and reflects real-world problems and tasks (Campbell, 2000). Brooks and Brooks (1993) described how to achieve greater learning by posing problems that are relevant to students. The use of projects developed over time rather than traditional tests also can give a much deeper measure of student learning. In addition to many of the ideas cited under the "constructivism" portion of this review, following are some examples of how technology can bring real-world problems to the classroom.

A gift of land to Blue Valley schools made it possible to develop a natural wilderness environment typical of Kansas prior to its settlement by farmers and the growth of suburbs and cities. One function of this area is to allow science students to study the habitat, food chain, and various life forms of a natural environment. Technology has allowed students to engage in a scientific investigation and data analysis in a real-world investigation with other students across the United States at the Globe Project website. The composite of data collected from similar sites nationwide provides insights into climate, water quality, and other environmental measurements across the United States.

General physical education classes in Blue Valley high schools learn much about their real state of health, not just the appearance of health that accompanies youth. A TriFit integrated online health evaluation system is connected to a computer that serves to process, store, and provide feedback on the data input from the TriFit device. The system measures strength, flexibility, and cardiovascular health. Students can provide information about lifestyle, diet, and so forth, and the system can give feedback on ways to improve health. Finally, the system develops an exercise program that can help a student improve his or her overall health and target specific goals for health improvement.

Blue Valley is a growing community that includes several suburban "cities," townships, and some unincorporated areas. A recent debate over the proposed annexation of a township by a suburban city prompted the creation of a WebQuest for high school sociology students (see www.bv229.k12.ks.us/bwest/favorites/webquests/urbansprawl/index.htm). In this project, students use websites and interviews to research the viewpoints of a variety of interest groups such as real estate developers, farmers, and environmentalists. The students make mock city council presentations for their researched perspective. They also collaborate in groups with students advocating the other perspectives to generate a recommendation for a growth plan for their community.

Although chat rooms might seem to be an unlikely tool for education, middle school students first began using chat-room software as a means of developing their word-processing skills and communicating with their peers in computer class. These students improved their typing skills as they passed messages back and forth with their classmates. At the same time, they learned about etiquette for online communication, differences between the business or academic environment and the personal or recreational environment online, and the district's acceptable-use policies. Students are aware that the chat log is saved and is used to provide students with feedback on their communications.

Contemporary communications students in the high school engage in a variety of projects that develop their communication skills and business or job skills. Students in the class evaluate marketing strategies in the media and then develop their own marketing products. Among these products is a three- to five-minute videotaped (edited using computerized digital video editing equipment) infomercial for a school activity, club, or sport. Another product is a three-column brochure designed to promote the activity.

In addition, a variety of content-specific courses focus on applying technology to real-world applications. The business department naturally uses computers for word processing, desktop publishing, Web publishing, and accounting. A course in the family and consumer science area called "Computers and Lifestyle Management" teaches students to apply technology to a wide variety of life situations. Students in the middle school use a variety of computer-based modules in the industrial technology area to explore computer-assisted design, computer-aided manufacturing, video editing, and more. In the high school, students use AutoCAD software to study drafting and architectural drawing. Students in the telecommunications and networking course have "contracted" with teachers in the schools as well as external clients for the development of websites.

A final example is a course called "Technology Support Practicum." The program allows students to learn about computer maintenance and repair and basic operations of software and computer networking. In addition, students study such concepts as customer relations, project and time management, and quality control. Students begin developing their skills before the school year actually begins by working with technology support staff and teachers in the district. During the semester-long course, they respond to technology support requests in their school; take turns providing "management" to the students in the program; continue their study and skill development by working with school staff; and select a major project involving research, software development, or something else that would be useful in school. Final evaluation involves presentation of projects to a panel at the end of the semester.

MEETING THE NEEDS OF DIVERSE LEARNERS

Addressing individual student needs can be accomplished by differentiating the learning activities used in the classroom and for student assignments (Tomlinson, 1999). Although both the theoretical foundation for "learning styles" and our understanding of brain function are still under development, research does support ways in which we can make a difference in student learning by carefully using these constructs and theories (Wolfe, 2001). Programs such as the "Technology Support Practicum," AutoCAD, and "Technical Physics" keep some students engaged in a way that traditional classes would not. In some cases, availability of these programs may keep students from dropping out. Some of these school experiences provide students with opportunities for independence and leadership. As these students provide competent computer support in a manner that recognizes teachers as "customers," teachers report that they see the students in a completely new light. Students report feeling valued and respected by the school in a way they never had before; their testimonials are an inspiration to provide opportunities for work on real problems in more ways throughout the curriculum.

Technology makes it possible to address the various learning styles of students more effectively. Presentation materials can involve multimedia data sources. Equipment such as musical keyboards, drafting tools, and digital cameras all allow students a hands-on experience with the curriculum through technology.

In addition to increasing the relevance of school, technology can help special-needs students to increase learning and independence. Several excellent examples of the use of technology to meet student needs arose from a T^3 grant (Learning Generations) with the University of Kansas. In one of these projects, teams of learners in a fifth-grade class designed presentations entitled "Opening the Doors to the New World." These students completed research using preresearched sites with authentic historical resources, graphics, etc., about the exploration that led to colonization by the Pilgrims. The unit (a WebQuest) culminated with student presentations during the Thanksgiving season. The WebQuest was prepared using the HPERTEC tool known as *TrackStar* (see the website at http://hprtec.org) to guide the students' research. The "frames" design of this website provided needed structure and assistance to students with varied skills at navigating the Internet. As students gathered their data, they used the computer software Inspiration to plan their project, generate a system of organization, and ensure that appropriate data was available for each area to be covered. Students with limited reading ability were able to participate in the research because e-Reader software allowed them to hear the text being read aloud. This software is useful in other academic areas as well. These students still work with the school's reading specialist, but the software allows them to participate in academic pursuits that once were impossible because of their reading difficulties.

CONNECTING WITH PARENTS

Parental involvement is yet another key element linked to increased student performance (Jones, 2001). Even schools that are struggling to close the achievement gap have found parental involvement to be a powerful tool for school improvement (NEA, 2000). Blue Valley has a history of using technology to make a connection with parents. Beginning with voice mail for all parents and teachers (long before voice-mail systems were commonplace), Blue Valley made it possible for teachers and parents to contact each other when work schedules made direct conversation difficult. By 1997, teachers were showing increased interest in creating class websites, and two years later, this interest was well documented in the 1999 self-assessment of teacher use of technology.

Although many teachers took the plunge and created their own websites, some opted to use the "cut and paste" approach with e-boards. More recently, the district created an easy-to-use tool that allows every teacher to have a personal Web page containing assignments, calendars of events, links to relevant sites, and a link to the teacher's e-mail.

PROFESSIONAL DEVELOPMENT

For over a decade, much has been written about the link between certain characteristics of staff development and resultant growth in student achievement (Joyce & Showers, 1988). Most recently, research has revealed the importance of linking pedagogical staff development with content area knowledge and skills (Sparks & Hirsh, 1997). Blue Valley staff members have embraced the technology, staff-development offerings, and the emphasis on content area practice. This is revealed through a self-assessment of technology use among teachers implemented in the spring of 1999 (Moore, Bartolac & West, 2000). Data from this assessment provided insight into how our staff were using technology, what they desired to learn, and how they wished to use technology in the future. This information helped us create and deliver targeted staff-development opportunities that would meet staff needs and conform with "best practice" in delivering staff development. In addition, our technology staff development team identified some critical items that may not have been listed among the staffs' priorities. For example, learning about acceptable-use policies and copyright are not thrilling topics, and it was no surprise that teachers were not clamoring for workshops on these topics. So each workshop and course was designed with these components embedded within the sessions. Although teachers indicated a desire to learn about presentation tools, we knew that going beyond presentation to uses of technology that were more than just enhanced lectures with a blackboard was our ultimate goal. Thus, workshops on PowerPoint included ways to put students at the center of the activity. Projects during workshops included the obligatory "back to school" show for parents but also emphasized how to teach students about the effective use of presentation tools and to make them the users of the technology rather than developing glitzy teacher lectures.

In 2001, the district readministered the self-assessment. The district found significant improvement in several outcomes targeted by their staff-development efforts. Staff members have made tremendous progress in creating personal Web pages for communication with home and students. They have increased their use of the Web for professional growth and still have a high level of interest in improving their use of technology.

CHALLENGES AND CONCLUSIONS

The successes experienced in Blue Valley in many cases support the recommendations made by Larry Cuban in his book *Oversold and Underused: Computers in the Classroom*. For example, he speaks to the importance of recognizing the expertise of teachers and valuing their critical role in the design and implementation of professional development. Such professional development should be designed after the model set forth by the National Staff Development Council to achieve actual classroom implementation of what is learned and to achieve any impact on student learning. Dr. Cuban points to the need to put computers to work enhancing best practices in teaching. Ongoing support for best practice can be supported by well-designed professional development and by day-to-day support of technology mentors, by classroom teachers given time to assist their colleagues, through team planning and study groups, etc.

In Blue Valley, teachers have been the primary designers and deliverers of technology professional development since the late 1980s. Working with the human-resources division, they have developed a comprehensive program of training that is matched to the interests expressed by teachers and that supports curriculum implementation and goals of individual buildings and the district. Each workshop or course engages teachers in producing materials both for use in their classrooms and for developing lessons that reflect the principles of effective instruction cited previously. Feedback from participants contributes to the improvement of the content and process in the training. Project and lesson ideas are also collected and shared with other teachers.

Technology must be both reliable and readily available if teachers are to make use of it. Teachers who plan a lesson around student research (making use of highly relevant, recent information, primary sources, a wider array of periodicals online, etc.) on the Internet, schedule the event in the lab or library, and then discover on the day of the experience that the network is down will be reluctant to design such a lesson again.

It might seem that there is never enough technical support, particularly when support of classroom technology is in competition with maintaining administrative computing functions. To increase the likelihood that technology actually works in classrooms and libraries in Blue Valley, cadres of technology support personnel (about 75 percent as many persons as there are school buildings) focus strictly on support of instructional technology. Additional staff members maintain the district's network and administrative computers, perform major repairs, etc., but the school-based cadres that work exclusively on the classroom and library hardware make it possible for teachers to trust that resources will be working when needed.

Technology must not simply add new skills to the rest of the curriculum, nor should it be used to simply add electricity to the same old methods for teaching and learning. To accomplish truly effective use, technology must be an integral consideration in the design of any curriculum, in the planning of any student project or assessment, and in the selection of instructional resources. It should then be embedded, where appropriate, in the professional growth activities that support the implementation of a curriculum revision (yes, there should be such inservice with any major revision of the curriculum). The example from Dr. Cuban's book about low use of technology in schools in Silicon Valley highlights the need for any infusion of technology to be accompanied by professional development equally infused with effective teaching practices and curriculum revision based on what we truly want students to know and be able to do and not simply what used to be convenient given limited nontechnological tools.

Classroom teachers with a deep understanding of effective instruction and technology are the key to supporting teachers in their integration efforts in Blue Valley. In addition to the staff-development programs discussed previously, two district coordinating teachers for technology (DCTs) are released full time to explore software, help teachers plan lessons, team teach, provide training opportunities within the school day and within classrooms, and work with every curriculum revision committee to consider available resources and instructional best practices. Several years ago, there was a perception among some in the community that high schools were doing less than elementary and middle schools to change practices and utilize technology. The response was to identify one classroom teacher (to be called a "technology integration specialist") in each high school to be released full time to provide similar support to the DCTs but focused in a single building. The response was overwhelmingly positive. In each case, the criteria for selecting these teachers focused on expertise as a teacher, demonstrated skill at effective technology integration, and rapport and ability to work with colleagues as a mentor. The most technologically sophisticated individual was not necessarily the best selection; an excellent teacher with good technology skills could grow in technology knowledge, but someone without strong interpersonal skills with colleagues would likely not succeed. People filling these various roles have included an elementary teacher, a middle school science teacher, a high school math teacher, a high school communication arts teacher, a librarian/social studies teacher, and two business teachers who had collaborated with other departments in teaching "contemporary communications." The synergy of this interdisciplinary group continues to contribute to their repertoire of strategies for technology integration and to their ability to help colleagues grow as teachers.

Dr. Cuban suggests that, unless we focus on desired outcomes and goals, supporters and critics of technology might some day agree that our investment has been wasted. He cites the view that technology often sits unused in schools, or that it is used only to automate old processes.

Having seen examples of effective use, we must ask, what makes the difference? Consider an analogy: A community wishes to build a bridge across a river to provide access for students to wonderful learning opportunities on the far shores. Political decisions are made and funding is collected, but the engineers warn that there is only enough money to build the bridge three-fourths of the way across the river. Still, the project proceeds. A few teachers decide to take their children to the brink, jump in, and swim the rest of the way to shore. These pioneers actually make good use of the learning experiences—just enough to cause the community and politicians to ask why all teachers are not using the bridge. A decision is made to widen the bridge so that more classes will have faster access to the resources. Again, money is collected and the bridge is widened and improved with attractive ornamental lighting (but it still only reaches three-quarters of the way across the river).

At times, this analogy accurately captures the frustration of those who see the possibilities of technology. Schools often don't have the resources to provide quality staff development. They often don't listen to the engineers (teachers) who could improve the design. At times, there is insufficient hardware or connectivity. In some cases, communities rush to provide student access at the expense of recognizing the absolute necessity for a teacher to have the tools to design learning experiences, explore resources prior to student use, increase efficiency in dealing with the mountains of paperwork, etc. What is most frustrating is that we know much about what it takes to do the job right in schools, but we'll only give a fraction of the effort required. In addition to the difficulties faced within schools, beyond the school walls some students have access to a wide range of learning opportunities while others have no such access in their homes or even in their communities. Then we question why students in one community seem to do so much better than those in others.

There is no doubt that funding is an essential element if the necessary hardware, staff development, and ongoing support are to be available. Despite a pattern of school funding in Kansas that caps the per-pupil expenditures in every public school and that has not even kept up with inflation for the last ten years, Blue Valley has used community support of school bonds to build up-to-date new facilities to keep up with rapid growth and to upgrade hardware and infrastructure of existing facilities. Frankly, this effort in Blue Valley to effectively use technology has been accomplished in spite of—not because of—support from the state of Kansas.

Even if statewide funding for technology was available, this would not be enough to ensure effective use of computers. District-level leadership is essential if teachers are to receive necessary support for change. Unless the vision for technology includes several crucial elements, the implementation will fall short. Blue Valley has been fortunate to have leaders with both vision for education and advocacy for effective practice. Bob Moore, director of information and technology since the early 1990s, approached the job with priorities that are not commonly held by IT directors. Rather than focusing on administrative applications of computing and making decisions based on convenience for technical operation of networks and systems, he made the first and foremost criterion for all decisions the impact the decision would have on teaching and learning. The superintendent of schools, Dr. David Benson, has internalized the vision and carried it to the board of education as a key component in a quality school district. Members of the board have also often been champions of technology and are willing to support the paths to success proposed by district staff. The person responsible for instructional technology has a focus on the real business of schools—teaching and learning—and has (for the most part) been empowered to advance that focus. Support has been systemic, from the superintendent and board throughout the organization.

The teacher's union has also been an essential contributor to success. Assigning classroom teachers to support technology integration ultimately adds to the overall staffing costs in the district; the teachers have recognized the value of this kind of support, however, and have advocated for these positions even if it affected overall monies available for salaries. Similarly, teachers want the technical support to keep the equipment working and consider such support a wise investment. When the district contemplated a teacher self-assessment of technology use, the union participated in its development and implementation, assuring staff that its purpose was to improve the schools and to support professional growth. It is worthy of mention that the positive relationship between district and union extends far beyond the field of technology integration. The union worked with the human resources department in the design of the new teacher induction program, proposed many of its elements, and advocated for "peer assistant" teachers to support novices in the profession. Again, there is systemic support for the quality of the school district and the strength of the teaching force from Blue Valley NEA President Sherrelyn Smith and throughout the leadership of the local union.

Success has ultimately been built on two basic elements: (1) the support of the schools, staff, and community exceeds whatever the state of Kansas would allow for schools and (2) teachers and administration have been willing to invest their time and energies in changing the way their schools do business. The commitment of these groups has made it possible to do a better job of building the technology bridge to the far shore—to more adequately fund the hardware and technical support and to engage in "best practice" in professional development and teaching and learning.

Sharing the successes and the paths to success is crucial if we are to gain needed support for change and funding. Students in the early grades through high school (and beyond) can find school to be highly engaging, can be encouraged to explore their world and construct essential conceptual understandings, and can develop relevant skills to deal with real and significant problems. Technology can empower teachers to create such school experiences for students. It can enhance the ability of students to dialogue, reflect, and participate as citizens in a democratic society. If we recognize what is possible and how to accomplish it, a few questions remain: Are we willing to invest what it takes to achieve these desirable goals? Are we willing to make these resources available to all students, regardless of their income level and where they live? Many dedicated teachers are committed to making a difference for kids and await the commitment of their communities to answer these questions affirmatively.

REFERENCES

Applefield, J., Huber, R., & Moallem, M. (2000/2001). Constructivism in theory and practice: Toward a better understanding. *The High School Journal, 84* (2), 35.

Brooks, J., & Brooks, M. (1993). *In search of understanding: The case for constructivist classrooms.* Alexandria, VA: Association for Supervision and Curriculum Development.

Campbell, D. (2000). Authentic assessment and authentic standards. *Phi Delta Kappan, 81* (5), 405–407.

Cone, D. (2001). Active learning: The key to our future. *Journal of Family and Consumer Sciences, 93* (4), 19–21.

Cuban, L. (2001). *Oversold and underused: Computers in the classroom.* Cambridge, MA: Harvard University Press.

Jones, R. (2001). Involving parents is a whole new game: Be sure you win! *The Education Digest, 67* (3), 36–43.

Joyce, B., & Showers, B. (1988). *Student achievement through staff development.* White Plains, NY: Longman.

Krajewski, B., & Parker, M. (2001). Active learning: Raising the achievement bar. *NASSP Bulletin, 85* (624), 5–13.

Marzano, R., Pickering, D., & Pollock, J. (2001). *Classroom instruction that works: Research-based strategies for increasing student achievement,* Alexandria, VA: Association for Supervision and Curriculum Development.

Moore, B., Bartolac, C., & West, B. (2000). How am I doing? *Electronic School,* at www.electronic-school.com/2000/01/0100f4.html.

National Education Association (NEA). (2000). *Making low-performing schools a priority: An association resource guide.* Washington, D.C.: National Education Association.

Shawhan, J. (1998). The Civil War online: Using the Internet to teach U.S. history. *Leading and Learning with Technology, 25* (8), 22–27.

Sparks, D., & Hirsh, S. (1997). *A new vision for staff development.* Alexandria, VA: Association for Supervision and Curriculum Development and Oxford, OH: National Staff Development Council.

Tomlinson, C. (1999). *The differentiated classroom: Responding to the needs of all learners,* Alexandria, VA: Association for Supervision and Curriculum Development.

Wolfe, P. (2001). *Brain matters: Translating research into classroom practice.* Alexandria, VA: Association for Supervision and Curriculum Development.

6

THE USE OF TECHNOLOGY THAT AFFECTS HOW TEACHERS TEACH AND STUDENTS LEARN

Thomas E. Pfundstein
Beachwood High School, Cleveland, Ohio

INTRODUCTION

Many people contend that we saw more technological advancement in the twentieth century than in all of the past centuries combined. Technological advancements from the atomic bomb to the computer have forced society to constantly change and adapt to the "new and improved" ways of doing, seeing, or hearing things. As we embark on a new millennium, it is safe to say that society has made a rapid transition from the Industrial Age to the Information Age. In the Information Age, people are bombarded with large amounts of easily accessible information. For example, a user who is researching a given topic on the Internet can obtain a huge quantity of information with a click of a mouse. The Information Age has transformed society into a global community in which people in distant places can communicate their ideas, cultures, and traditions to one another.

Recent technological advancements pose a challenge for today's educators. Thus far, the Information Age seems to have made peoples' lives more efficient, but we must constantly learn new skills to keep up with the rapid pace of change. It seems that as soon as we learn a skill, it becomes obsolete, and we must learn a newer skill. Skills that have been taught for years in the educational system are fast becoming outdated.

To prepare their students to succeed in the Information Age, today's educators must teach students to critically analyze and manage vast amounts of information.

This chapter discusses how educational technology can affect the way students learn and the way teachers teach and offers some ideas about how technology can be deployed to transform teaching and learning. If planned and implemented properly, technology can provide a positive learning experience for students and educators.

Part one of this chapter describes how one school district attempted to implement technology in its curriculum; part two discusses the resources that are needed to successfully implement technology into its curriculum. In part three, I cite the critical challenges that must be met to use technology successfully in pre-K–12 education. Finally, in part four, I describe some of the ways in which educational technology has changed how I teach and how my students learn. In this last section, I also define Web-based instruction (WBI) and explain what I see to be the advantages and disadvantages of WBI in a pre-K–12 setting.

The sources for this chapter are two documents[1] that were part of the application process for national awards of excellence, the current literature on WBI, and my own observations and experiences with WBI.

BEACHWOOD CITY SCHOOL DISTRICT AND TECHNOLOGY

The Beachwood City School District[2] is located in a small upper-middle-class suburb on the east side of Cleveland, Ohio. Many consider Beachwood to be one of Ohio's finest suburban settings. This city of 14,000 takes pride in being a blue-chip business center, a thriving commercial and shopping area, and a national leader in technology. The residents of Beachwood are predominately well-educated professionals who understand the value of education and expect excellence in their children's schools.

The Beachwood City School District includes five schools that serve 1,693 students in grades K–12. Ninety-six percent of these students are college bound. Compared to national averages, class sizes in Beachwood schools are small. In the elementary schools, there are about twenty students per classroom; most classes at the high school have fewer than twenty students. In addition to the core academic subjects, foreign languages are taught from kindergarten through the twelfth grade. Among the many special programs offered are programs for learning disabled students in grades 1 through 12 and programs for gifted students in grades 4 through 8. The Total Communications program serves deaf and multihandicapped high school students in the area.

In recent years, the Beachwood City School District has received local and national awards. During the 2000–2001 academic year, the district met twenty-six of the twenty-seven state of Ohio performance standards. In June 2001, *Cleveland Magazine* rated Beachwood City Schools the number one school district out of sixty-five districts in northeastern Ohio. In the spring of 2000, the Beachwood Middle School became the first school in the state of Ohio to win a second national Blue Ribbon award. Finally, both the high school and middle school have earned an Excellence in School Management Award from the William M. Jones/Harvard Business School Club of Northeastern Ohio. The award recognizes outstanding school leadership and management in northeastern Ohio. Some of the factors that have enabled Beachwood to achieve so many local and national awards are a teacher-pupil ratio of 11.9, an annual per-pupil expenditure of roughly $15,000, and outstanding student performance demonstrated by some of the best test scores in the country.

The faculty at Beachwood City Schools averages thirteen years of teaching experience. Seventy percent of the faculty holds a master's degree or a Ph.D. Each of the five school buildings has librarians; reading specialists; art, music, and physical education teachers; and building tutors. In addition, counseling services are available for all students in grades K–12.

In the past five years, the Beachwood City School District has made a concerted effort to incorporate more technology into its curricula. The resources necessary to implement technology into the curricula include the implementation of hardware and software, visionary school leadership, and technology support. At the start of the 2000–2001 academic year, the district had more than 700 computers with Internet connectivity. Each of the five schools has at least one centralized computer lab, with three labs in the high school and two labs in the middle school. The high school and middle school are each equipped with wireless computer labs that are available for teachers and students to use in various areas in their respective buildings. Because of the district's commitment to technology, the National School Board's Association Technology Network has ranked the district in the top one-half of 1 percent nationwide in the use of technology in an educational setting.

The Beachwood City School District has standardized hardware and software to ensure reliability. Students in grades K–8 use and are taught computer skills using iMacs and wireless iBooks. Students in grades 9–12 have access to both Macintosh and Windows platforms in class and in lab settings. For word-processing software, all secondary and middle school students, faculty, staff, and administrative personnel use Microsoft Office. Elementary students use Appleworks 6.0, the latest version of word-processing software from Macintosh. Administrators have computers equipped with conversion software that allows them to easily switch documents from Macintosh to Windows platforms. Beachwood's interschool communication software is the FirstClass system. FirstClass provides each administrator, faculty member, staff member, and student with a district e-mail account that is accessible from school or home via downloadable software or the Web. The system also allows each faculty and staff member to complete online forms (absences, field trips, work orders, etc.), hold online conferences, back up files, maintain an online calendar, and design and upload independent Web pages.

THE IMPORTANCE OF ESTABLISHING STANDARDS

The impetus to implement technology in Beachwood City Schools began about five years ago with the development of a districtwide technology strategic plan. Spearheading the plan were a visionary administration and school board and a handful of teachers who realized the importance of educational technology in transforming the way students learn and the way teachers teach. The technology plan is based on national and state technology standards.[3] To ensure the successful implementation of technology throughout the district, the plan identifies five standards:

1. Every student will use technology to access, organize, analyze, and communicate information to improve the learning process.
2. Technology will be used to develop competent, technologically knowledgeable staff.
3. Available technology will be utilized for districtwide management and global communication.
4. District technology will be made to create lifelong learning opportunities for all segments of the community.
5. The district will collaborate with community agencies to enhance the school's technology program.

Each of the five standards contains objectives with specific action steps that are necessary to the incorporation of technology districtwide.

The high school principal, who also serves as the district's technology coordinator, heads the technology committee. The Technology Advisory Committee meets once a month to address instructional alignment strategies for implementing technology into the curriculum. The committee consists of technology teachers from each building, a school board member, the network administrator, and district support staff.

Technical support and maintenance are crucial to the success of the implementation process. The district has incorporated a cost-effective technology plan for purchasing equipment and support services as needed. The schools also have access to in-house support and technical assistance through an automated Intranet-based Helpdesk. The network administrator has his office in the high school and is accessible to faculty and staff. Technician specialists are part of the district's Rotating Assistance for Technology (RAFT) network, which provides technical support and training in the various school buildings throughout the school week. The instructional technology department also employs two part-time assistants. One assistant is in charge of a certified in-house Apple repair service, and the other is directly responsible for the district's technology purchasing.

INFLUENCING THE WAYS TEACHERS TEACH AND THE WAYS STUDENTS LEARN

The district's continuous effort to implement technology in the curriculum has had a profound impact on teachers, students, and community members, namely parents. Many teachers in the school district design and maintain class websites. In general, teacher-created Web pages contain course information and content, assignments, and links to a host of educational resources for students and parents to access at school and at home. Some teachers in the district use Internet-based software, such as Blackboard.com, to provide course content and self-assessments to their students. By making course materials available to students and parents online, teachers are extending the classroom outside the confines of the physical structure of the school building. For example, when students are absent, they can readily access the daily assignment or class notes from home provided they have Internet access at home.[4] The Internet has also had an impact on how teachers deliver instruction. Using an LCD projector connected to a computer, teachers can develop and deliver interactive lessons, such as WebQuests and collaborative online projects. Teachers can also take students on virtual field trips to museums and other places of interest or access maps or primary sources for students to analyze.

In the Beachwood schools, technology has affected the way students learn in two important ways. First, the implementation of technology into the curricula promotes an active approach to learning. Some students learn best through hands-on activities. Unlike a traditional classroom in which students typically remain seated and receive information from the teacher, in a technology-enhanced approach, students are actively engaged in the content by way of the computer. Although they remain seated during most of the class period, they are active both physically (using the mouse) and mentally (gathering and analyzing information).

Second, the use of technology in schools fosters a student-centered approach to learning. In *Horace's Compromise*, Theodore Sizer (1992) suggests that our educational system should promote a student-centered, rather than a teacher-centered, approach to learning. Student-centered learning can be defined as occurring when the amount of student discussion of learning tasks is equal to, or greater than, the amount of teacher talk; when instruction is individual or in small groups; when students participate in determining the rules of the classroom; and when instructional materials are available for students to use individually or in a group (Spring 1994, p. 244).

Through the use of technology, students are literally in control of the primary learning tool, namely the computers. Students view the computer as the mechanism that provides them with the information they need to construct meaning. In one teacher's interactive classroom, students can sit anywhere because each computer is connected to a server; thus, students can log into any one of the twenty-four computers in the class. Once students log in, they are able to change certain features on the control panel of the computer to personalize it according to their own specifications. For instance, the teacher allows students to insert their own photos or scenic pictures on their desktops. Having their own pictures gives students a sense of ownership of the computer and makes them realize that they do in fact have some control over what goes on in the classroom. In effect, the teacher is surrendering some classroom control by providing students with choices and allowing them to make decisions about their own learning (Ames, 1992).

WBI also fosters a student-centered approach by individualizing the learning process. By posting assignments on the Web, students are able to work at their own pace. Once a student has mastered one assignment, he or she can move on to the next. Students who are having difficulty with the assignment know that the instructor is available to assist them. This is extremely effective in a classroom where students have a wide range of academic abilities. By allowing students the opportunity to work at their own pace, the instructor is able to move freely throughout the class, facilitating instruction. Also, through the Web, the instructor is able to provide both enrichment and remedial assignments for students to complete.

The implementation of technology has increased communication between the school and parents in four ways. First, the district website provides parents and community members with updated information, such as bulletins from the principal, contacts, schedules, and school links. Second, the Internet gives teachers a way other than the telephone to communicate with parents. Through e-mail, parents are able to ask teachers about their children's progress. Third, one teacher uses an online testing program and is able to forward (via e-mail) results of an exam to parents immediately after it is taken. The teacher claims that parents especially like this feature because it allows them to track their children's progress. Fourth, through the Internet, teachers are able to post assignments and grades for parents to view. In some instances, students might tell their parents that they have no homework or that an assignment has been canceled. With a class website, parents can log on at any time and see what is due and when it is due. This helps get parents involved in their children's educational lives. At all times, parents can know exactly what is going on in their children's class. This may help spark at-home discussions between parents and their children. If WBI is used properly, it is a communication tool that can help build continuity between the school and home.

BARRIERS TO IMPLEMENTING TECHNOLOGY

In *Oversold and Underused: Computers in the Classroom* (2001), Larry Cuban describes how various educational institutions have spent large sums to get schools wired and prepared for the Information Age. Cuban argues that although these schools are fairly well prepared for the new era, they need to do more than simply purchase hardware and software if they expect technology to have a profound impact on teaching and learning. Although Cuban singles out a few examples in his study where the use of technology in schools is altering teaching and learning, he believes that most members of the educational community have not significantly changed their approaches.

Not all of the teachers and students at Beachwood have embraced the implementation of technology into the curriculum. Although I am convinced that Beachwood schools are at the forefront in educational technology, they, like most schools across the country, still face many challenges. The technology challenges that face Beachwood can be grouped into three areas: hardware and software, faculty-related, and students.

Although Beachwood places a high priority on purchasing computer hardware and software, the district must resolve three problems if it is to successfully continue the technology initiative it began five years ago. First, not all members of the school community have the same number of computers in their classrooms. For example, some teachers have a computer for each student in the classroom, whereas others have only one computer for the entire class. Also, these computers do not all have the same capabilities. This presents a problem because even if a teacher wants to implement technology in the classroom, he or she might not be able to either because there are not enough computers or because computers lack sufficient capability. Second, maintaining and upgrading the hardware and software is a major concern. The district has only one full-time employee and three part-time employees in the information technology (IT) department. Furthermore, the maintenance person visits each school only once each week. This causes problems when, for example, a piece of equipment fails on Tuesday, and the maintenance person is not scheduled to return until the following week. Third, when using technology in the classroom, it is imperative to have a back-up lesson in case the computers are down. For example, one teacher complained that she had worked hard on a Web-based lesson, but on arriving at school was told that she would not be able to use the lesson because the network was down.

In regard to implementing technology in the curriculum, the teachers at Beachwood face four major challenges. First, like most teachers across the country, they take on additional responsibilities within the school such as coaching and advising student organizations. Because of this, it is hard to fit technology training into their busy schedules. Even when teachers attend the initial professional development sessions, it is difficult to arrange the necessary follow-up training that they need to fully understand the technology. Furthermore, teachers are often daunted by the rapid pace of technological change. Many teachers feel that no sooner do they learn one set of skills than it is time to learn another. The second challenge is that some teachers are not comfortable with the fact that computers promote a student-centered approach to learning in which the student has some degree of control over the instructional medium and learning process. For some traditional teachers, it goes against the grain that the integration of technology promotes the role of a teacher as a facilitator, not as a disseminator of knowledge.[5] Some teachers simply refuse to change the way they teach because they believe that what they have been doing has been effective over the years. A third challenge is that schools have historically been people-oriented institutions in which teachers and students engage in face-to-face interaction throughout the school day (Picciano, 1998). With computers, there is less face-to-face interaction, and this bothers many. Finally, teachers who make consistent use of technology in their classrooms must be on guard that the technology does not overshadow the content that is being taught.

The implementation of technology presents students with three challenges that teachers must be aware of within the confines of their classrooms. First, computers and the Internet can distract a student's attention. Getting and keeping their students' attention is of utmost concern to most teachers. With all the games and commercial websites that are available to students, teachers must ensure that students stay on task when they are working on the computer. Second, the abundance of information available to students on the Internet may result in information overload. On a given topic, students are exposed to a plethora of information that must be analyzed for its educational appropriateness. For example, a simple Internet search on the subject of the Civil War will produce a long list of websites. Students must be taught media literacy and critical thinking skills. Third, some students have problems using technology in the classroom because they have not had the appropriate training. These students often become frustrated because their resistance to technology inhibits their learning process.

Two additional challenges that educators face in regard to implementing technology into the curriculum are financial constraints and limited educational research that supports the use of educational technology. It is no secret that it costs an enormous amount of money to implement and maintain educational technology. If a school needs money to repair its building or hire new staff, funds often come from the technology budget. In addition, little research has been done on the effectiveness of educational technology in a pre-K–12 educational setting. This is particularly true with a newer technology, such as WBI.

WBI: WHAT IS IT?

At the center of the Information Age is the World Wide Web (WWW). In recent years, the use of the WWW has grown at an exponential rate. Some estimates suggest that the use of the WWW is increasing between 6 and 20 percent per month (Ritchie & Hoffman, 1998, p. 1). Although most people spend their time "surfing" the WWW in an informal manner, it can also serve as an excellent instructional tool in the classroom. When properly structured, the WWW can guide users through a series of instructional activities that present information, offer practice exercises, and provide suggestions for remediation and enrichment as well as feedback to inform the users of their strengths and weaknesses (Ritchie & Hoffman, 1998, p. 1). Use of the WWW is becoming increasingly popular in schools. According to the U.S. Department of Education (2001), by the fall of 2000, 98 percent of the country's public schools were connected to the Internet. Now educators must challenge themselves to learn how to use the WWW to provide positive learning experiences for their students and prepare them for their future role in a technologically specialized society.

The recent growth of the Internet has opened up an entire new area of academic research. There is no single definition of what Web-based learning is, but two definitions seem to capture its implications. One is "the application of a repertoire of cognitively oriented instructional strategies implemented within a constructivist and collaborative learning environment, utilizing the attributes and resources of the World Wide Web" (Relan & Gillani, 1997, p. 43). A second is "a hyper-media based instructional program which utilizes the attributes of the World Wide Web to create a meaningful learning environment where learning is fostered and supported" (Khan, 1997, p. 2). Although these definitions capture important aspects, WBI also fosters a student-centered approach to learning.

WBI provides numerous advantages that a traditional teacher-centered approach cannot provide. According to Scholz-Crane (1997) of Rutgers University, some of the advantages that WBI offers students and teachers are (1) a learner-centered approach, (2) interactivity, (3) multimedia exposure, (4) immediate delivery of information, and (5) all with minimal technological skills. I would also add that WBI (6) makes an efficient teacher and (7) provides real-life skills.

WBI is student-centered in that it places the student in charge of the instructional tool, namely the computer. WBI is interactive in that students are active participants in the learning process, unlike in the traditional classroom setting where they sit and absorb the information that the teacher is disseminating. WBI offers a wide range of multimedia components that focus on various learning styles. Through the use of the computer, students can easily access audio, video, and hypertext to meet their specific learning styles. WBI offers just-in-time delivery of information. For instance, if a news story breaks during the middle of the school day, students can log onto the Internet and get the full information at the click of a mouse. This is especially effective in social studies, where current events play an integral role in the curriculum. The Internet is relatively easy to use. It does not require a great amount of technological skill. In other words, participants do not need to be computer programmers to use WBI; all they really need is a computer and an Internet connection. When using the WWW as an instructional tool, teachers are able to create an easily retrievable database of their information. They no longer have to continually make copies and file information in manila folders. Rather, their information is stored and is available to them and their students at the click of a mouse. Finally, as society becomes increasingly technologically driven, WBI provides students with real-life technical skills that will be useful throughout their educational careers, as well as in their future professions.

Along with its many advantages, WBI has some important drawbacks. First, in WBI, face-to-face interaction is reduced because the computer stands between the instructor and the student. Certain factors such as facial expression, conversation, and tone of voice are taken out of the educational process. Second, even though the number of Internet connections is growing at a rapid pace, the Internet is not available to everyone. Third, not all computers have the same capabilities; thus what loads quickly on one computer may take a long time on another. Finally, WBI can create problems in classroom management. For example, teachers often have a hard time monitoring the work that students are doing on the Web. Some are truly engaged in learning, but others are simply "surfing" the Web to check out their favorite websites. There is also the question of student accountability. For instance, a student might receive an assignment from another student and try to turn that assignment in as his or her own. Although these disadvantages are cause for concern, the WWW can still be a highly effective learning tool if it is used properly.

There are two approaches to WBI. One is called *synchronous WBI*. In a synchronous environment, the collaborative learning that occurs is done in real time (Driscoll, 1998, p. 52). Students meet at a specific site and use the WWW as an instructional tool (distance education).

In a synchronous learning environment, students are presented with poorly structured problems that require synthesis and evaluation of information and shared experiences (Driscoll, 1998, p. 52). The role of the teacher is to facilitate learning and offer assistance when needed. The second approach, asynchronous WBI, offers learning that occurs at different times and places. In an asynchronous setting, the less structured problems require application, analysis, synthesis, and evaluation (Driscoll, 1998, p. 52). An example of an asynchronous learning environment would be a course taken over the WWW in which students did not meet on campus but completed the required work when it was convenient for them. This type of learning has become extremely popular at the university level. With Internet-based software applications such as FirstClass, Blackboard, Aspire, and Web-CT, instructors are able to place their entire curriculum online in an attempt to instruct and assess students. In fact, at the University of Akron, one could earn an M.B.A. online without ever setting foot on campus.

IMPLEMENTING TECHNOLOGY IN THE CURRICULUM

My interest in using the WWW as a medium for instruction began for selfish reasons, but I quickly realized that it offered many educational benefits for my students. Five years ago, I was teaching social studies at a large suburban high school. Being the new teacher in the department, I did not have my own classroom and was forced to carry all of my materials on a cart and switch classrooms just like the students. I was also required to provide copies of my lesson plans, assignments, and assessments to various resource teachers throughout the building. Frustrated by these many demands, I set out to find a way to make my curriculum more easily accessible to those who needed it. My search ended with the Internet. I could devise a way to place my curriculum on the Internet, and then anyone who was interested could retrieve the materials anytime. During that same year, I began to develop a course website that would host my curriculum on the Internet, but I soon found that the school did not have the technologies that I needed to incorporate a Web-based approach.

The following year, I accepted a teaching position at a small suburban school district that was on the verge of implementing technology in its curriculum. The entire district was networked to the Internet, and each member of the district had his or her own e-mail accounts. This was the perfect opportunity for me to implement my ideas. Having no formal training in instructional design, I had my share of difficulties, but over time, I have developed what I believe to be a Web-enhanced course that incorporates both a synchronous and an asynchronous approach to learning. Furthermore, I think that the Web-enhanced course has beneficial implications both for me and my students.

To help implement my Web-enhanced course, the school district invested significant funds in an interactive classroom. The interactive classroom has twenty-four iMac server-based student computers that are connected to the Internet. The computers are individually housed under glass-top desks. The computers are placed under glass for two reasons: First, the flat top of the desk provides students with an area to perform traditional schoolwork, such as reading and writing, and second, the placement of the computers is ergonomically correct. In other words, the position of the computer allows students to maintain proper posture while working on the computer, thus relieving stress from their necks, backs, and eyes. Each desk is also equipped with a keyboard tray that slides under the desk and locks into place when in use. The position of the desks allows the instructor to see students' faces and enhances the personal communication between students and the instructor.

A teacher station is situated in front of the classroom. The teacher station is equipped with a G3 Macintosh, which is positioned under a flat glass top with a pullout keyboard tray. The computer is connected to a projector, which is situated on the ceiling in the middle of the classroom. The projector has a wireless mouse, which allows the instructor to move freely around the room without losing control of the main computer. Furthermore, multimedia components, such as a VCR and DVD player, can also be connected to the projector. To the side of the main computer is a scanner, which is used by both the instructor and students.

My first step in implementing the Internet into my classroom was the website, which I designed (and currently maintain) during the 1998-1999 academic year to make the curriculum available to students, parents, and resource teachers.[6] On the website's home page, there are eleven buttons that link to information as it relates to the social studies courses I teach. I have found that the class website offers many advantages. Students, parents, and resource teachers are able to access the social studies curriculum from school and home. When students are absent, they can check the website for assignments or the notes they missed. Parents can keep up with their children's academic progress by checking their grades online and by seeing what assignments are due and when. The class website gives resource teachers access to assignments to help those students who have special needs. I use the website as an in-class instructional tool to foster authentic learning experiences. For example, if I am doing a lesson on the Revolutionary War, I am able to guide students to relevant websites that offer virtual field trips to battle sites and museums.

Another way in which I integrate the Internet into the classroom is by using the district's intranet system, FirstClass. FirstClass enables faculty members and students to communicate with one another online, as well as with the outside world. Although e-mail is an integral component of the system, FirstClass has numerous other online features. Using First-Class, I have established conferences to extend the learning opportunities outside the classroom. Conferences are online mailboxes that allow the instructor and students to post messages asynchronously. Using the conferences, I post assignments and discussion topics that students respond to when convenient. Through these threaded discussions, students are able to interact with each other about social studies content, both synchronously and asynchronously. In a sense, I am taking my class beyond the parameters of the physical classroom. In addition, through FirstClass, I am able to provide students with online assessments, such as objective tests and surveys that provide immediate feedback to the students and to me.

MEETING THE NEEDS OF DIVERSE LEARNERS

Recent research on intelligence suggests that human intelligence is more than simply an IQ score (Sternberg & Kaufman, 1998). One such theory, formulated by Gardner (1983), suggests that humans have multiple intelligences. According to Gardner, "there is no single, unified intelligence but rather a set of relatively distinct, independent, and modular multiple intelligences" (Sternberg & Kaufman, 1998, p. 492). In Gardner's original theory of multiple intelligences, humans have eight intelligences: linguistic, logical-mathematical, spatial, kinesthetic, musical, interpersonal, intrapersonal, and naturalist. (Gardner has added two other intelligences: spiritual and existential.) Although Sternberg and Kaufman caution educators about Gardner's theory of multiple intelligences (Sternberg & Kaufman, 1998, p. 493), Gardner's theory sheds light on the notion that students learn in different, distinct ways.

In today's classrooms, the make-up of the student population is extremely diverse. Although *diversity* can refer to race, culture or ethnicity, and gender, for the purposes of this chapter I use *diversity* to refer to learning styles. I contend that WBI supports an effective means for reaching students with various learning styles. A traditional lecture format does not provide those students who are visual learners with the optimum way to learn. In a lecture-based class, visual learners need visual clues to help them understand the material. Often, information is not properly processed when a teacher simply lectures to the class. However, in WBI, much of what is being taught is visually represented on the computer screen in front of the student. Thus, students who do not adequately process what the instructor is saying could be aided by a visual representation on the computer. Through the WWW, I am able to link to websites that provide visual representations of the points I am attempting to make.

The use of WBI is especially effective when dealing with students with special needs, especially deaf students and English as Second Language (ESL) students. Using a network management system known as *Desktop Assistant* (Apple), I am able to interact with deaf students through a synchronous chat. If a deaf student does not fully understand a point, he or she can send me a message to which I can directly respond without the assistance of a translator. This is extremely helpful to the deaf students because they are able to keep both the lesson and the virtual chat open on their screens. They do not have to move their visual attention to the translator, which could cause them to lose some of what is being stated. With deaf students, the lines of communication are more direct between teacher and students.

WBI can also help ESL students. For example, if a student cannot aurally understand what I am saying, I can provide the pertinent information on the Web, which the student can then translate into his or her primary language. A few years ago, I had three students from Korea, all of whom benefited from WBI. They could barely understand what I said in the classroom, but having the curriculum available to them on the Internet gave them the time they needed to read the material and translate the information if necessary.

WBI also seems to have a positive effect on the learning process of audio learners. Through the use of audio software, such as Real Player and QuickTime, students who learn best aurally are able to hear the material that I may be presenting in a visual manner. In a given lesson, I may convert my lecture notes into a sound file, which allows students to listen to the material. If I am teaching a lesson on Martin Luther King Jr., students who are audio learners can benefit from listening to a sound byte of the speech on the Web. Placing sound files on the Web can have an enormous impact on those who have problems with phonics as well. Having reading materials available to them through oral means allows them to listen to the sounds and words and may help with pronunciation without the assistance of a resource teacher. Through headphones, audio learners are also able to listen to content material in such as way that it does not bother the rest of the class.

There are two other ways that WBI can reach students with various learning styles. First, WBI promotes an active approach to learning. Some students learn best through hands-on activities. Unlike a traditional classroom where students typically sit and receive information from the teacher, in WBI, students are actively engaged in the content by way of the computer. Although they remain seated during most of the class period, they are active both physically (using the mouse) and mentally.

Second, WBI assists students who, because of their interpersonal skills, learn best through collaboration. Using WBI, students are able to actively engage in learning experiences with other students. Blumenfeld calls this type of collaboration peer learning (Blumenfeld et al., 1996). Through the use of the computer, collaboration can occur within a class, among groups in a class, and with people and groups outside the classroom (Blumenfeld et al., 1996, p. 39). Blumenfeld also claims that emerging technologies, such as the WWW and e-mail, can increase collaboration in an educational setting (Blumenfeld et al., 1996, p. 39). In my classroom, I attempt to implement collaborative experiences. Through online conferences, students are able to discuss topics pertinent to the content by way of threaded discussions. Threaded discussions are grouped messages that members of the conference can respond to synchronously, or asynchronously. If students have a question about a topic, they can send a message to the conference, and all students (as well as the instructor) can view it and offer a response.

PROMOTING COLLABORATIVE LEARNING

In my experience thus far, there are four positive aspects to this type of collaborative communication. First, online conferences enable students to interact with all members of the class, not simply those within the classroom. In other words, students in one period are able to collaborate with students in another. In addition, through group-sharing software, I am able to establish online collaborative projects in which students can work collaboratively with members from other classes and even other schools. Such projects might be close to impossible without the aid of the computer and the Internet.

Second, according to Blumenfeld, "experience indicates that students who do not typically engage in classroom discussions participate in these computer-based, classroom-wide conversations" (Blumenfeld et al., 1996, p. 39). Students who are shy or feel intimidated voicing their opinion in front of their peers actively engage in online discussions. In addition, students can self-edit their ideas and choose their words more thoughtfully during online conversations.

Third, online collaboration enables students to respond to a topic when it is convenient to them. Through asynchronous threaded discussions, students are able to post responses as long as they have Internet access. I have found this to be extremely useful for students who are having difficulty with an assignment they are doing at home. Rather than relying on a few friends, students can post a question to the conference for all other participants to view. More often than not, by the time the student returns to school, he or she has received a response from me or from another student (this is especially effective over the weekend or extended vacations). Through synchronous conversations, I am able to provide my students with continuous learning experiences outside the walls of the school. For example, I often have live chats with my students the evening prior to an assessment. These online review sessions enable students to question me, as well as other students, about the material. These sessions are often convenient for both the students and me because we are often too busy to meet for an after-school review session.

Fourth, through WBI, students are able to evaluate each other. Peer evaluation can be an effective learning tool in teaching writing skills. In my classroom, I often have students comment on other students' work through online conferences. For example, students can post an essay to the conference. Then I will have them analyze another student's response by sending that student a personal e-mail with a critique. Students then receive alternative perspectives on the topic and as immediate feedback. Furthermore, I would posit that when students know that their peers will be reading a piece of writing, they tend to be more careful in their writing process because they want to show others that they have an understanding of the task. In sum, WBI provides an optimum way to provide positive learning experiences to a wide range of learning styles. It is not suited to every learning style, but it can provide an optimum way to help most students learn in a way that is best for them.

TECHNOLOGY'S ROLE IN MOTIVATING LEARNING

WBI can also be used as a motivational tool to foster learning. In an age of instant gratification, the task of motivating students seems more challenging than ever. Students are surrounded by distractions, and teachers are always searching for ways to motivate their students, both extrinsically and intrinsically. It has been my observation that WBI helps motivate students in the learning process in numerous ways.

Simply using the computer to learn a content area makes some students excited about learning. When students enter the classroom and know that they will be using the computer to learn social studies, their interest is often aroused. Initially, students might simply want to use the computer, but with the proper guidance, they soon realize that they can learn about history—and learn about it in an exciting way.

Also, by the nature of its design, WBI motivates students. Through the use of the Web, students are exposed to colors, animations, sounds, and graphics that, at least initially, capture their attention. The use of these external stimuli can all be added to a Web page to motivate students (Ritchie & Hoffman, 1998, p. 1). In addition, the Web draws students' attention to it through its use of these external stimuli. If properly developed, websites can keep students attentive during the learning process. Students' ability to move from one site to another at a relatively fast speed keeps them wondering what will come next.

Finally, with WBI, learning is fun. Students enjoy being on the Internet in an attempt to construct meaning. There are numerous online activities to engage students, such as WebQuests, virtual field trips, games, and simulations. Intertwined in the curriculum, these online activities can provide positive learning experiences and be fun as well.

CONCLUSION

Contrary to Cuban's findings in *Oversold and Underused*, some school districts have successfully used technology as an educational aid. With the proper planning, technology can be used to transform teaching and learning. Although the financial and human investment of educational technology may be large at the outset, the implementation of technology is essential as educators prepare students for the challenges that will confront them in the Information Age. I have attempted to show how one school district has begun to implement technology into its curriculum. Although Beachwood schools are at the forefront in the use of educational technology, they still face crucial challenges that must be addressed before the full possibilities of certain educational technologies can be realized. I have also attempted to explain WBI through the literature and my own experiences. Although there is no definitive definition of WBI, one of its striking features is that it provides students with a learning environment that is far different from traditional methods of instruction. When used properly, WBI can be an effective learning tool. Through my research and observations, I am convinced that WBI is an excellent tool to help students with the learning process. Although relatively little empirical research has been done on the effects of WBI and student learning, the field is wide open for investigation by academics and practitioners. Furthermore, the subject must be examined further to determine whether the large sums of financial and human resources required by WBI are worth the investment for teaching and learning. It is my hope that, in the future, learning theory specialists, technology specialists, and educators will collaborate to determine the effectiveness of WBI.

NOTES

1. These two documents are part of the application process for the Blue Ribbon Schools Program (2001–2002) and the Ohio Award for Excellence (2001).

2. For more on the Beachwood City School District, visit the school website at www.beachwood.k12.oh.us.

3. State standards are outlined by Ohio SchoolNet (http://www.ohioschoolnet.k12.oh.us/home/) and the national standards provided by ITSE (http://cnets.iste.org/).

4. Most Beachwood students have at least one computer at home, which facilitates the integration of technology.

5. By traditional I mean a teacher-centered approach.

6. For a preview of my website, visit http://www.beachwood.k12.oh.us/~tep/home_page.html.

REFERENCES

Ames, C. (1992). Classrooms: Goals, structures, and student motivation. *Journal of Educational Psychology, 84* (3).

Blumenfeld, P. C., Marx, R. W., Soloway, E., and Krajcik, J. (1996). Learning with peers: From small group cooperation to collaborative communities. *Educational Researcher, 25* (8), 39.

Cuban, L. (2001). *Oversold and underused: Computers in the classroom.* Cambridge, MA: Harvard University Press.

Driscoll, M. (1998). *Web-based training.* San Francisco: Jossey-Bass Pfeiffer.

Gardner, H. (1983). *Frames of mind: The theory of multiple intelligences.* New York: Basic Books.

Khan, B. H. (1997). Web-based instruction (WBI): What is it and why is it? In Badrul H. Khan (Ed.), *Web-based instruction* (pp. 5–18). Englewood Cliffs, NJ: Educational Technology Publications, Inc.

Khan, B. H. (Ed.). (1997). *Web-based instruction.* Englewood Cliffs, NJ: Educational Technology Publications, Inc.

Picciano, A. G. (1998). *Educational leadership and planning for technology* (2nd ed.). Englewood Cliffs, NJ: Prentice Hall.

Reidl, J. (1995). *The integrated technology classroom: Building self-reliant learners.* Needham Heights, MA: Allyn & Bacon.

Relan, A., & Gillani, B. (1997). Web-based instruction and the traditional classroom: Similarities and differences. In Badrul H. Khan (Ed.), *Web-based instruction* (pp. 41–46). Englewood Cliffs, NJ: Educational Technology Publications, Inc.

Ritchie, D. C., & Hoffman, B. (1998, June 6). *Rationale for Web-based instruction,* at http://edweb.sdsu.edu/clrit/WWWInstrdesign/Instruction.html.

Scholz-Crane, Ann. "Creating Effective Instructional Modules for the World Wide Web." Paper presented at Computer in Libraries '97, 1997.

Sizer, T. R. (1992). *Horace's compromise: The dilemma of the American high school.* Boston, MA: Houghton Mifflin.

Spring, J. (1994). *American education.* New York: McGraw-Hill.

Sternberg, R. J., & Kaufman, J. C. (1998). Human abilities. *Annual Review Psychology, 49,* 36–65.

United States Department of Education. (2001, December 1). *Report on Internet and Schools,* at http://nces.ed.gov/fastfacts/display.asp?id=46.

7

ENSURING THE IMPACT OF TECHNOLOGY ON SCHOOLS AND SCHOOL-AGED CHILDREN: THE K^{12}NECTS PROJECT IN FAIRFAX COUNTY PUBLIC SCHOOLS

Diane S. Reed
Fairfax County Public Schools, Virginia

Using technology in public schools is an expensive proposition. The nation has spent nearly $50 billion on e-rate subsidies and other federal, state, and local initiatives over the past decade. As a result, technology use in schools has taken a quantum leap. Not all school systems, of course, can afford heavy investment in the hardware, software, and training that are required to make technology work for their students. School systems must weigh the relative value of technology use against other pressing needs. Professor Larry Cuban has argued persuasively that technology is getting in the way of other important educational goals by being "oversold and underused." His position cannot be taken lightly, yet his conclusions are premature. What American public schools need now are credible plans to implement technology and to investigate what does and doesn't work, and what the human and material costs of our decisions vis-à-vis technology in schools are.

This chapter describes how one relatively affluent public school system in the eastern United States is trying to build a new model for implementing and investigating technology use in its own schools by providing the essential conditions that are likely to change teaching and learning.

BACKGROUND

Fairfax County, Virginia, is one of the leading technology centers in the country. With its highly trained and well-educated workforce, and close proximity to Washington, D.C., Fairfax County is considered the "Home of the Internet." More than 50 percent of worldwide Internet traffic passes through Northern Virginia every day. Fairfax County is home to more than 4,000 technology firms, and it employs 175,000 people in knowledge-based companies—nearly one in three jobs countywide. It is also headquarters to some of the world's leading technology companies (Fairfax, 2001). Fairfax County Public Schools is a large suburban school district that has 234 schools and centers and 165,016 students. It is the twelfth largest school district in the United States. In 1999, 93 percent of its high school graduates went on to some form of postsecondary education. All classrooms are wired for Internet connectivity, and the school system is currently completing the final phase of Internet content filtering. Fairfax County has set three major objectives as part of its long-term strategy in technology planning: (1) superior student learning through technology, (2) effective and efficient teaching and school management through technology, and (3) effective and efficient school division operations through technology (FCPS, 2001).

WHAT GETS IN THE WAY OF TECHNOLOGY IMPLEMENTATION?

There are obstacles that make the successful implementation of technology especially challenging. These include, but are not limited to, access, teacher practice, support, central planning, and vision and leadership. These obstacles, which reasonable people—both advocates and detractors of technology use—consider important, are difficult to overcome.

THE K¹²NECTS PROJECT—BUILDING A MODEL

To address the district's technology objectives, Fairfax County administrators must understand the relative influences of inputs, processes, and outputs of technology on teaching and learning. The K^{12}nects project (pronounced "con-nects") is an attempt to help them in this effort. It is a public–private partnership between Fairfax County Public Schools and the Fairfax County Public Schools Education Foundation. The Foundation secured the involvement of leading technology providers as corporate partners. The eight partners—Microsoft, Cisco, Dell, Compaq, Tandberg, CMS, ISmartT, and HP—have pledged more than $6 million in products and services.

The school division is committed to using technology to improve teaching and learning and has spent almost $4 million in infrastructure, support staff, and hardware in its target schools. This project is an attempt to develop a K–12 prototype in which technology is used to support educational best practices and to investigate links between technology and student achievement. The K^{12}nects project will try to answer the question: "Why does technology work in some schools and not in others?" The goals of the project are to give ubiquitous access to high-end computing devices and provide to students an environment of fully integrated technology-supported instruction, authentic inquiry-based learning, customized instruction, and the ability to extend the learning opportunities beyond the classroom into the home and the community (Dunning & Rosebush, 2001).

The K^{12}nects project is to be implemented in seven schools. The high school has 1,700 students, the middle school has 950 students, and the five elementary schools accommodate 375 to 850 students each. In addition, there are centers for gifted, deaf and hearing-impaired, and learning and emotionally disabled students, as well as for adult literacy and community education programs. The schools in this "pyramid" support an English for Speakers of Other Languages (ESOL) population that represents more than forty different nationalities. Minority students make up 28 percent of the enrollment. Roughly 7 percent of the students qualify for free or reduced-price lunches.

PLANNING FOR TECHNOLOGY

The K^{12}nects project staff has used the enGauge Model of thinking about learning, teaching, and leading in the digital age to guide their work. The North Central Regional Educational Laboratory and the Metiri Group developed the model. EnGauge provides a framework of critical factors deemed to be important influences on the effectiveness of learning technology. The six essential conditions of enGauge are:

1. forward-thinking shared vision
2. educator proficiency
3. effective teaching and learning practices
4. digital age equity
5. robust access anywhere, anytime
6. systems and leadership

The enGauge online survey measures a school's progress in each of the essential conditions (NCREL, 2000). Keeping these conditions in mind, the school administrators, technology specialists, and teachers in this project were asked to think of technology use in new ways. In past models of technology implementation, the schools were passive recipients of technology. A fixed number of computers were delivered to the schools, a fixed amount of training was given, and then they were left on their own. K^{12}nects requires an action orientation. Each school in the project establishes a K^{12}nects team. This group of teachers, administrators, and parents shape school objectives and technology use meant to address their objectives and the state standards of learning.

The enGauge website consists of three major components:

1. A framework for understanding the systemwide factors that influence the effective use of educational technology.

2. An online assessment tool that districts and schools can use to measure systemwide effectiveness. Online surveys and offline assessment instruments translate the six essential conditions into measures of effectiveness.

3. A menu of "high impact" technology-based resources matched to a school's and/or an individual's profile.

www.ncrel.org/engauge/
(NCREL, 2000, no. 5)

CHANGING TEACHER PRACTICE

In 1998, the Commonwealth of Virginia commissioned the Milken Exchange, SRI International, and the North Central Educational Laboratory to study technology use in the Commonwealth. Surveys, site visits, and focus groups were conducted throughout the state. One of the findings of this report states: "The Commonwealth's K–12 students and educators are gaining expertise in basic computer skills but generally are not yet using technology effectively to improve student learning" (Milken-Exchange-NCREL, 1999). K^{12}nects is a response to that concern. Fairfax, via enGauge, is shifting the focus from simply using the technology to improving student learning. The school division is doing so with the clear understanding that technologies alone rarely bring about substantial change in teaching and learning (Bennett, et al., 2000).

The project staff pays special attention to effective teaching and learning practices and educator proficiency. K^{12}nects is using the LoTi Profile to assess classroom teachers' current level of technology implementation. LoTi, developed by Christopher Moersch, attempts to measure authentic use of technology in classrooms. This scale focuses on the use of technology as an interactive learning medium, assuming that that interaction makes the greatest and most lasting impact on classroom pedagogy and also is the most difficult to implement and assess (Moersch, 2001).

Christopher Moersch developed LoTi (Levels of Technology Implementation) in 1994. The challenge is not merely to use technology to achieve isolated tasks such as word processing a research paper, creating a multimedia slide show, or browsing the Internet, but rather to intergrate technology in a way that supports problem-solving, performance-based assessment practices.

/www.learning-quest.com/LoTi/
(Moersch, 2001, no. 10)

The LoTi assessment was given at the beginning of the project to all teachers and administrators. Results will guide professional development for the school and will provide baseline data for assessing progress toward the goal of technology integration. The

LoTi framework uses seven levels of implementation, ranging from nonuse (level 0) to refinement (level 6). As teachers progress from level to level, changes in instruction are observed, and the instructional focus shifts from being teacher-centered to being learner-centered. Traditional verbal activities are gradually replaced by authentic inquiry related to a problem or a theme (Moersch, 1995). From the results of this online assessment, professional development can be designed to assist teachers to move to the next level of technology implementation. Each school principal is able to get an aggregated report of the school data. Cuban suggests that more than half of elementary and middle school teachers continue to be nonusers of computers for classroom instruction; when teachers do adopt technological innovations, they typically maintain rather than alter their existing classroom practices (Cuban, 2001). Fairfax is attempting to prevent this dilemma by monitoring teacher practice. The LoTi scale actually helps teachers to direct more learner-centered and problem-based approaches and assists them in moving to the next level of technology implementation (Moersch, 2001).

The seven levels of technology implementation used in the LoTi assessment are shown in table 7.1.

TECHNOLOGY SUPPORT

To provide "just-in-time" support for teachers, Fairfax County Public Schools has placed a full-time school-based technology specialist (SBTS) in each of the target schools. These specialists play an integral role in mentoring, training, and planning with the staff. The SBTS staff hold nonteaching positions, and their primary responsibility is teacher training. They are available to provide individualized support and group training to teachers in their own classrooms and to help them integrate technology into their instructional programs. Along with the SBTS support, Fairfax County provides technology support specialists (TSSpecs), who assist the schools and the SBTS personnel in addressing technical problems. This support team is viewed as critical to the successful implementation of technology in the schools.

Table 7.1.   Levels of Technology Implementation (LoTi)

Level 0	Non-Use: A perceived lack of access to technology-based tools or a lack of time to pursue electronic technology. Existing technology is predominately text-based (e.g., ditto sheets, chalkboard, overhead projector).
Level 1	Awareness: The use of computers is generally one step removed from the classroom teacher (e.g., integrated learning system labs, special computer-based pullout programs, computer literacy classes, central word processing labs). Computer-based applications have little or no relevance to the individual teacher's instructional program.
Level 2	Exploration: Technology-based tools serve as a supplement to existing instructional programs (e.g., tutorials, educational games, simulations). The electronic technology is employed either as extension activities or as enrichment exercises to the instructional program.
Level 3	Infusion: Technology-based tools, including databases, spreadsheets, graphing packages, probes, calculators, multimedia applications, desktop publishing applications, and telecommunications applications, augment isolated instructional events (e.g., a science-kit experiment using spreadsheets/ graphs to analyze results or a telecommunications activity involving data-sharing among schools).
Level 4	Integration: Technology-based tools are integrated in a manner that provides a rich context for students' understanding of the pertinent concepts, themes, and processes. Technology (e.g., multimedia, telecommunications, databases, spreadsheets, word processors) is perceived as a tool to identify and solve authentic problems relating to an overall theme or concept.
Level 5	Expansion: Technology access is extended beyond the classroom. Classroom teachers actively elicit technology applications and networking from business enterprises, government agencies (e.g., contacting NASA to establish a link to an orbiting space shuttle via the Internet), research institutions, and universities to expand student experiences directed at problem solving, issues resolution, and student activism surrounding a major theme/concept.
Level 6	Refinement: Technology is perceived as a process, product (e.g., invention, patent, new software design), and tool to help students solve authentic problems related to an identified real-world problem or issue. Technology, in this context, provides a seamless medium for information queries, problem solving, and/or product development. Students have ready access to and a complete understanding of a vast array of technology-based tools.

TEACHER PRODUCTIVITY

Cuban's general assertion that technology has failed to change teaching and learning practices may be premature. In any event, Fairfax County Public Schools' Instructional Management System (IMS) is an attempt to effect change. The IMS provides all teachers in IMS schools with the tools to improve student achievement through the use of formative student data, the use of high-quality resources, and the application of "best

practice" instructional strategies. When the system is fully implemented, it will also provide parents and administrators of IMS schools
with access to information they need to partner with teachers to improve student learning. As each school is brought into the IMS, the
school infrastructure is upgraded to 100-Mb access to every desktop, a
second T1 line, and a high-end workstation on every teacher's desk. The
IMS software helps align the curriculum to state standards and national
frameworks, and when fully populated will automatically generate tests
and analyze test items. Teachers will be able to customize the learning
for individual students.

UBIQUITOUS ACCESS TO TECHNOLOGY

By the end of the first year of the project, K^{12}nects will make available nearly 300 HP Jornada Pocket PC handheld computers for students. Three elementary schools each selected one sixth-grade class,
the middle school selected one entire "team" of 150 students and
seven teachers, and the high school selected one class of ninth-grade
social studies students to receive these computers. Handheld computers can be used in a variety of ways. They serve as calculators,
notepads, digital cameras (with an attachment), or scientific sensing
devices. Their low cost makes them a reasonable alternative to laptops and desktop computers. Students can use the devices to store,
process, and retrieve information. Handhelds provide the feeling of
ownership and can be a true "personal computer" (Pownell, 2001).
Teachers in the K^{12}nects project are using the Jornada as a tool for
classroom management and to further the goal of teaching students
organizational skills. Teams of students collaborate and "beam" their
papers to each other in their writing groups. Dell Wireless labs are
also being used to provide access to technology. These mobile labs or
carts are equipped with fifteen laptop computers and wireless Internet access, which can be moved from classroom to classroom. Students and teachers are able to move these wireless laptops around the
room to solve the problems of furniture and space and encourage student collaboration.

E-LEARNING

"The good news is that the Internet is bringing us closer than we ever thought possible to make learning—of all kinds, at all levels, any time, any place, any pace—a practical reality for every man, woman, and child" (Commission, 2000).

Changing the paradigm of the "brick and mortar" school to a virtual learning space is another focus of K^{12}nects. E-learning is changing the face of education today. Fairfax County Public Schools is using a commercially purchased platform to establish an e-learning environment. Students have the opportunity to access class materials anytime to extend the learning day, and anyplace to extend the classroom. The online learning environment allows teachers to add graphics, sound, and video; to have asynchronous and synchronous collaboration tools to communicate with their students; and to do formative assessments. This new environment gives learners multiple paths for understanding and enables teachers to provide differentiated assignments. This online platform is also a way for parents to partner with the school in the child's education. We have known since the Coleman report of 1966 that the home variable is at least as important as the school (Wehlburg, 1995/1996). Another aspect of e-learning is videoconferencing. All K^{12}nects schools have videoconferencing systems by TANDBERG and are participating in a project with schools in Northern Ireland, a learning opportunity that brings children around the world together in collaborative learning experiences. The partnership with schools in Northern Ireland was begun at Mantua Elementary School and has spread throughout the pyramid.

FORMAL ASSESSMENT

Planning for the initial assessment of this Fairfax County Public Schools initiative is focused on two areas: the state of Virginia Standards of Learning (SOL) scores and the enGauge survey. The End-of-Course Virginia Standards of Learning scores in high school sciences in a target school will be compared to a school that has not had the technology infusion of the K^{12}nects schools. The enGauge assessment of parent and teacher attitudes and perception of educational technology use in their school will be described using survey results. (This online survey is available free of charge at http://www.ncrel.org/engauge/.) The parent profile captures parent involvement and perceptions of technology use in their children's schools. The educator profile on enGauge is intended to capture not only specific technology skills but also educator proficiency with planning, implementing, and assessing technology-supported learning with students. Data generated from these surveys yield a mean score in each of the six areas of enGauge interest (NCREL, 2000). The K^{12}nects project staff, principals, and teachers will also participate in focus groups. Data gathered from all these sources will serve as grist for the construction of case studies that will describe influences of technology on students, teachers, and learning. Later phases of assessment will include direct classroom observations of teachers' classrooms as they use technology with and for their students.

CRITICAL CHALLENGES

Most of the teachers in the K^{12}nects schools have ubiquitous access to technology. If teachers were asked whether technology has affected their teaching, most would probably answer, "yes." Few, however, have made major pedagogical changes in their teaching and classroom organization. Many use the computer as a presentation device for PowerPoint, or to project a test, or to show their class objectives. Especially in the upper grades, "teacher-centered" delivery is the most common mode of instruction. Shifting the focus of instruction to a more student-centered approach and increasing student ability to solve problems and demonstrate competency over challenging subject matter, particularly in mathematics and science, are major challenges. Teachers who use computers to engage students in their own learning are far fewer in number. They involve students in identifying and solving a problem. In short, these teachers support students in their efforts to engage in activities and generate products relevant to student goals. Presumably, when students work with problems that relate to their personal experiences, they are more likely to be motivated to think critically. Cognitivists as far back as Dewey have argued also that students who pursue their interests are more likely to seek deep under-standing of subject matter and to make conceptual connections among clusters of topics across related domains. Using success in this age of standards is challenging. Do the state-mandated SOL tests measure the real impact of technology? Will the effects of technology imple-mentation show up on the SOL tests? Are there better ways to mea-sure success? Certainly, academic standards and the assessment of those standards are important to policymakers. But so, too, is the cre-ation of opportunities for students to do more writing, more problem solving, and more engagement with real life—all skills that are not measured by these norm-referenced standardized tests (Rockman, 2000). K^{12}nects schools are working to find new ways to assess stu-dents' research skills, problem-solving abilities, and capacities to cre-ate interesting and useful products.

CONCLUSION

Complex problems resist simple solutions. It is easy and cheap to shoot from the hip, but the value of technology for students is beginning to be explored. Few technology implementations have been planned with many essential conditions in mind. We need to take the time and do the hard work necessary to judge technology use fully and fairly as we build educational models for schools, teachers, and students.

REFERENCES

Bennett, Dorothy, McMillian-Culp, Ketie, Honey, Margaret, Tally, Bill, & Spielvogel, Bob. (2000). It all depends: Strategies for designing technologies for change in education. In Heineke, Willis, Blalsi (Eds.), *Methods of evalu-ating educational technology* (Vol. I, pp. 105–124). Greenwich: Information Age Publishing.

Commission, Web Based Education. (2000). *The power of the Internet for learning.* U.S. Department of Education, at http://interact.hpcnet.org/webcommission/index.htm.

Cuban, L. (2001). *Oversold and underused: Computers in the classroom.* Cam-bridge, MA: Harvard University Press.

Dunning & Rosebush. (2001). *K¹²nects networking education: Community-teachers-students funding proposal*. Fairfax, VA: Fairfax County Public Schools.

Fairfax, County of. (2001). *Fairfax County Economic Development Authority*, at www.fairfaxcountyeda.org/ (accessed 31 October 2001).

FCPS. (2001). *Fairfax County Public Schools FY002 Technology Plan*. Fairfax: Fairfax County Public Schools.

Milken-Exchange-NCREL. (1999). *Report on the status of education technology availability & usage in the public schools of Virginia*. Santa Monica, CA: Milken Exchange on Education Technology.

Moersch, Christopher. (1995, November). Levels of Technology Implementation (LoTi): A framework for measuring classroom technology use. *Learning and Leading with Technology, 26,* 40–43.

Moersch, Christopher. (2001). *LoTi. National Business Education Alliance*, at www.learning-quest.com/LoTi/ (accessed 16 November 2001).

North Central Regional Educational Laboratory (NCREL). (2000). *enGauge*. At www.ncrel.org/engauge/ (accessed 10 November 2001).

Pownell, B. (2001). *Getting a handle on handhelds*. National School Boards Association, at www.electronic-school.com/2001/06/0601handhelds.html (accessed 24 November 2001).

Rockman, S. (2000). *A lesson from Richard Nixon: Observations about technology policy and practice in education,* [Web page]. U.S. Dept. of Education, at www.ed.gov/Technology/techconf/2000/rockman_paper.html (accessed 27 December 2001).

Wehlburg, Catherine. (1995/1996, December/January). The future of high school success: The importance of Parent Involvement Programs. *The High School Journal, 79,* 125–128.

8

THE IMPACT OF TECHNOLOGY INTEGRATION AND SUPPORT FROM COACHES

Diane Bennett

Mt. Juliet High School, Tennessee

INTRODUCTION

Mt. Juliet High School is located in Middle Tennessee about twenty minutes from Nashville. In many ways, we are an atypical secondary institution in a middle-class community. Our enrollment for the 2001–2002 year was 1,261. (Our enrollment dropped roughly 38 percent when a new high school recently opened in our county.) The ethnic composition of the school is roughly 94 percent Caucasian and 4.5 percent black, with the remainder being Hispanic, Asian, and Native American. For the last seven years, our graduation rate has hovered around 91 percent. Our student body is highly mobile; during the 1998–1999 year, 19 percent of our students either withdrew from school or transferred in or out. About 2 percent of our students receive free lunches. Our students' composite score on the ACT for the 1998–1999 year was 19.8, which is 0.1 percent below the state composite score, and 1.2 percent below the national composite score. We operate the typical school day on a four-by-four block schedule with ninety minutes of instruction in each class.

Each teacher has a computer in his or her classroom for administrative purposes, but under present school policy, students are not allowed to use these computers. Students are allowed to use special computers that have been installed in the vocational classrooms and in several other classrooms as well. In our four computer labs, 115 computers are available for student use. Three of these labs are associated with our business and vocational education curriculum and have classes scheduled throughout the day. The fourth lab, which has thirty computers, is available to teachers for technology integration. In the library, twenty-seven desktop computers are available for individual or classroom use. In the fall of 2001, the school system purchased 300 TI-83 graphing calculators for use by Algebra I students and others. Each teacher has access to the Microsoft Office suite and to E-Class, a computer program for grade management, attendance, and reporting. In addition, personnel throughout the school system have access to Microsoft Outlook, which has done much to improve communication.

Using money received from a Technology Literacy Challenge Fund (TLCF 2001) grant, the school bought fifty wireless laptop computers, three mobile security carts, three printers, three access points, three routers, an LCD micro miniprojector, and a digital camera. The school also bought enough software and training supplies to conduct an extensive on-site training program for the seventy-one staff members who are directly involved in student learning.

AVAILABLE TRAINING

To comply with our TLCF grant requirements, we are now training all full-time teachers and any part-time teachers who ask for training. (We have several part-time faculty members who divide their time between Mt. Juliet and the new high school.) Rather than train all of our teachers at once, we chose to train in small groups over the course of the year. Each group consists of ten to eleven teachers, two or three from each department, who are at roughly the same skill level. Each teacher is teaching twenty-four hours of training, along with a three-hour afternoon session of reflection.

In our training program, we focus on the major components of professional development that we addressed in our proposal, all of which correlate with our school improvement plan. During the training sessions, teachers create and implement standards-based engaged learning activities using wireless laptop computers.

As teachers go through the four-day training program, they plan and design one lesson consisting of specific criteria for a class of their choosing. The lessons they plan are much like those described in Goal 2 of Larry Cuban's book, *Oversold and Underused* (2001, p. 70). The ultimate goal is to design lessons that transform teaching and learning into an engaging and active process that is connected to real life. Proof that many of our teachers have succeeded in this effort can be found at http://www. wcschools.com/mjhs/tlcf/bestpractices.index.htm, where these lesson plans are posted. Teachers incorporate the use of Microsoft Office and other business software into their lessons. By working with software that is widely used in the business world, our students are gaining marketable skills that will serve them well in the future (Cuban, 2001, p. 16).

We have found that creating these lesson plans requires a level of understanding that is vastly different from what is required in other types of training in effective teaching practices. In this program, teachers must analyze learning experiences in great depth, breaking them down into components that show how technology can be used before reassembling them into a new version appropriate for their classrooms. We do this as a group during the training sessions. Creating these lesson plans gives teachers a sense of satisfaction because they are producing a useful product and, at the same time, are learning new technology skills. The lessons they plan typically engage students in cooperative learning groups and use technology in a student-centered task related to specific Tennessee Curriculum Standards. This is quite similar to the example of teacher Alison Piro in Cuban's book (2001, p. 14). As a technology coach, I have done a significant amount of Internet research on engaged learning and technology integration in an effort to help teachers design exemplary lessons.

TEACHERS APPLYING KNOWLEDGE IN CLASSROOMS

After their training sessions, our teachers search the Internet for activity-oriented, resource-rich ideas to enhance their lessons. I try to show them how they can adapt technology to their current lesson plans, and they seem to enjoy using technology tools to enhance lessons they have already prepared.

Each teacher is asked to participate in five, three-hour after-school staff development activities. We will offer approximately fifteen activities this year, and teachers may choose the ones that interest them most. Each teacher will have the opportunity to take up to forty-two hours of technology-focused training; we expect to offer close to 3,000 hours of training over the course of the year.

In our training program, we are stressing performance-based technology activities that are aligned with Tennessee Curriculum Frameworks. Teachers are asked to plan three instructional lesson plans that include the use of the Internet, as well as Windows, Microsoft Office suite, or other software that maximizes the use of our desktop and wireless labs. Our math teachers are also using the TI-83 calculators purchased with monies unrelated to this grant. Teachers are using our network to create and store files that their students may access and modify. Few teachers knew how to use our network resources before this grant was awarded, but now many teachers are using Word, PowerPoint, Excel, and the Internet extensively. Students are learning to work in teams, and some teachers are creating interdisciplinary units of study. Our teachers are using a variety of teaching practices that, taken together, are having a positive effect on students. Teachers are encouraged by the fact that their students are responding with enthusiasm.

Our district now has a countywide e-mail server. Teachers are using e-mail extensively, even those who were initially reluctant to do so. As a result, communication has improved, and this has made it easier for teachers to share resources. Students are using e-mail in their classroom assignments, but we do not have student e-mail addresses available through our network e-mail server. Teachers who are using e-mail to enhance learning projects are using Web-based e-mail accounts. Our administrators correspond regularly by e-mail both within the school and throughout the county.

Using the wireless laptop computers purchased with this grant has helped teachers feel a sense of professionalism. This is cutting-edge technology for schools in our state, and it gives us a sense of pride. Our teachers like being able to take a laptop home with them so they can practice what they learned in training, and they like having the opportunity to attend training sessions with their colleagues. A regular lunch out and a paid stipend for after-school work are a welcome break in the routine and do much to raise morale.

A portfolio is created for each teacher with an individualized printout of his or her skill level as of May 2001, when data were being gathered for our original proposal. Teachers also analyze what skills they need to improve upon and choose specific activities that will allow them to meet their goals. They use a four-step rubric to access levels of basic skills and technology integration in their classes. They analyze their progress in meeting their goals in a working document in their portfolios.

ROLE OF THE TECHNOLOGY COACH

As a technology coach helping to implement the grant, I am present in the classroom when a teacher uses the new technology for the first time. I feel this makes the teachers comfortable but also encourages them to present an exemplary lesson. I make certain they understand that I am there to provide support, not to evaluate their ability to teach. Being able to immediately apply their training in the classroom has been a positive experience. Skills are taught and demonstrated to teachers and students at the same time. Everyone, including the technology coach, is an active learner.

I see teachers using many different teaching strategies, and this has helped me improve my own teaching style. Too often, teaching confines us to four walls, where we become isolated in our own domain. Because we are collaborating during training and sharing those experiences, we are breaking barriers and opening new avenues of communication so that we can learn from each other. This is different from the usual dialogue in the teachers' lounge. The ability to participate cohesively and share our experiences as a group has been a highly productive part of this training.

To minimize the disruption of a teacher's being out of the classroom four days in a row, the training is given in two sessions, two days one week and two days the next. Having two sessions is beneficial for another reason: Teachers have a chance to think about what they learned in the first session before coming back the next week. Between the two sessions, teachers check with me and with mentors, tossing around ideas they have for using technology with their subjects and trying to formulate a plan that will work for their students. When they return to training, we have a chance to talk over those ideas with the group before turning to new ones.

After all the teachers in a particular training group have implemented their lessons, we gather once again to share our experiences. In what I call our "reflection and collection" meeting, we discuss what worked and what didn't. Teachers talk about their accomplishments and their failures and ask questions about anything they didn't understand in the training. During this reflection process, we learn things from each other that will make our next lessons more effective. I also collect their documents so that we can prove we have met our benchmarks and used best practices. All teachers have access to all lessons on our network and receive a CD at the end of the year.

We have had to make adjustments for the different training groups. For example, one group might ask to cover subjects that are not of interest to other groups. Because the training groups consist of only ten or eleven teachers, I can be flexible and give individual attention to each teacher. This small class size fosters group cooperation. I often meet with the teachers during their planning period to give them added help in personalizing their training. Although the training has specific goals, personalizing the training for each teacher builds their confidence.

At the end of each training group, I ask teachers to evaluate their training experience. From the evaluations, I have received many ideas that I have been able to implement in the groups that followed. A few teachers felt so overwhelmed by all there was to learn that they asked us to offer more training in the summer to reinforce the concepts they learned during the school year. Even teachers who are technologically skilled would like to have opportunities in the summer to plan departmental websites and develop other resources that could be shared with their colleagues.

EMPOWERMENT FOR TEACHERS AND STUDENTS

After implementing one wireless technology lesson, teachers are encouraged to implement two more lessons using the desktop computers that are available in our labs and in the library. They are also encouraged to reserve the wireless lab again and to use any other means of technology available. Nearly all the teachers gain confidence with practice, and we hope they will attempt more than these first three lessons. This may be hard to do, however, because resources are limited and teachers cannot always reserve the equipment when they would like.

The training program gives teachers options and choices. It doesn't confine them to a particular teaching style, but it does require them always to focus on state curriculum standards. Because teachers are in the best position to determine what they need to learn, I present a variety of teaching strategies that allow them to analyze the needs of their own students and, at the same time, focus on a standards-based approach. For this reason, I do not sense a lot of resistance from the teachers. Teachers enjoy the training because they are able to make choices and collaborate with other teachers in the training group. My biggest task this year is to help teachers see that technology is not a threat to their teaching style but instead offers an opportunity to improve it. Making that shift in thinking has encouraged some teachers to be bold in their strategies; it has scared others to death. As a school, the results we are seeing in our students, as well as in our teachers, spur us to do more. We all realize, however, that to be truly successful, this must be an ongoing process, not a one-year event.

I have observed that once teachers have empowered students by using technology, they want to do it again, and so they dig deeper, planning and implementing more teaching strategies that will help their students learn. It is the love of seeing our students discover new things that drives us to discover more ourselves. A school whose staff development program can inspire and encourage teachers to make new discoveries will enjoy success that lasts far beyond this pilot program.

"Lesson Plan Workshops" focus on the designing of lesson plans and allow teachers to build on their earlier training. This is beneficial because teachers would have already been introduced to the design process and would not have to worry about finding substitute teachers or dealing with classroom obligations as they did during the training year. Next fall, these teachers will be eager to use these lesson plans they have constructed themselves, and will be inspired to make even greater use of technology.

TEACHERS HELPING EACH OTHER

We are using departmental mentors to help teachers who are just beginning to acquire technology skills. Unlike Cuban's unexpected finding that teachers showed little evidence of technophobia, we do have a few teachers who feel that their teaching style is threatened by the use of technology (2001, p. 132). In my opinion, their fear stems from the uncomfortable feeling of having to move from teacher-centered to student-centered learning, as I encourage them to do in the training program. Teachers who are serving as mentors are slowly convincing these reluctant colleagues that they must get on board because technology offers such tremendous opportunities for change. Our mentors are teachers who have learned on their own or have taken brief courses and workshops and are already using technology in the classroom, much as described in Cuban's book (2001, pp. 56–57).

As we have moved forward with training groups, it appears that teachers are starting to collaborate with each other, sharing experiences and raising questions. Technophobia is being reduced, although it will be some time before it disappears completely.

We have used e-rate funding to supplement our efforts to go wireless. We have purchased additional access points so that individual laptops can be used in classes without the need to roll carts to the rooms. We can now use wireless computers in any part of the building that has a local area network (LAN) connection. Some teachers would like to purchase more access points so they can have continuous wireless connection in their classrooms and not have to reserve machines. This would be a tremendous help in seamlessly integrating technology because technology would be available on an as-needed basis.

CRUCIAL ROLE OF COMMUNICATION

We have tried to make our business community aware of our program. On the Channel 9 broadcasting network, we promote our experiences with the TLCF grant, and our program has been featured three times in local newspapers. Our demonstrations of the wireless network at parent-teacher conferences have prompted considerable interest from parents and teachers alike. We hope to have an adult education "orientation" night in the spring. Teachers from surrounding schools are aware of our efforts and want to know what is happening. Several principals have asked if I would have time to give after-school programs for their teachers.

Our faculty is kept informed of our progress as we move from month to month. We use e-mail to announce meetings and new learning opportunities. At every faculty meeting, I am asked to give an update on the training program. We post a weekly journal on our website that includes snapshots of teachers and students using technology during the week. The journal has been a huge success. Everyone likes seeing his or her picture. I am always amazed that as I take pictures, students are fully focused on their computer screens. They are on task; I don't ask them to pose.

I have also provided an extensive staff development website with resources to help teachers before, during, and after they go through training. We recently posted our "best practices," including our process for selection, the rubric used in evaluating the practices, pictures of exemplary teachers, detailed lesson plans, files used in presenting the lesson, samples of students' work, the teachers' analyses of the lessons, and other details. Each teacher selected for his or her "best practice" receives an engraved clock and has a chance to win a personal Dell laptop computer. This computer will be awarded in May to the "Technology Improvement Plan Team Player of the Year." This competition has unified departments and promoted a great deal of pride. Our faculty has commented that it is the best staff development program they have ever been involved in.

One of the most beneficial aspects of our program has been working with students on the student technology committee. These students provide input into how teachers can best reach them. In other words, they talk, and we listen. These high school students will soon enter college or the world of work, and they need to be challenged. We asked them to sit in on classes where technology is not being used and think about how technology could be used to enhance their learning of that lesson. They then share those ideas with me, and I, in turn, pass their comments on to teachers by way of our website and staff development programs. This process is changing the way teachers think, and it is allowing us to do a better job of reaching students. Students and teachers are encouraged to innovate and work cooperatively. Also, students know their teachers have been involved in a computer-training program, and they appreciate the fact that teachers are willing to learn new concepts. Teachers have told me their students sometimes give them "pep" talks before they head off to the training room. Students are quite nurturing to teachers who are "technophobic." We are collecting data that will tell us how often technology is being used and how it has affected individual classes.

CHALLENGES

Implementing a professional development program for technology integration presents a number of challenges, which have given substance to the theory that computers are "oversold and underused" in our educational institutions. Following is a discussion of a few of the problems we have faced in our pilot program at Mt. Juliet High School.

First, the program requires me to be both mentor and coordinator. Dealing with the logistics of scheduling and maintaining equipment and all the problems associated with malfunctioning computers is a huge job in itself. In my role as technology coach, I have been able to help teachers design lesson plans and provide minimal technical support as well. These are time-consuming responsibilities. We all wonder what will happen when we go back to our full-time teaching jobs at the beginning of the school year.

I have depended on our county's technology department to help me with the start-up and maintenance problems I cannot handle. At times, when I have been unable to get the technical support I need from the technology department, our operations have been virtually shut down. Sometimes we must wait days for assistance, which forces us to go to plans B, C, D, and beyond. When this happens, teachers lose their motivation to learn new skills. Teachers will never be able to fully implement technology until they are confident that the equipment will work when they want it to work. That again signals the need for on-call technical support that can quickly meet the needs of the classroom teacher. Cuban mentions the importance of this in his book (2001, p. 164). Even though people in our building are making fewer calls to the technology department because I am available full time, we need a better system of technical support. Teachers are beset by demands and have no time to deal with equipment that doesn't work properly. We don't expect businesses to operate without adequate support, and we shouldn't expect our schools to either. Until teachers are convinced that the equipment is reliable, they will be reluctant to use it regularly. Investing in technology without offering training and technical support is equivalent to buying a car and not considering the need for gasoline and tune-ups. However, if teacher training is handled properly and technical and curriculum support is available full-time, I disagree with Cuban's findings that teachers who have technology resources readily available will simply use technology to maintain classroom practices rather than alter the way they teach (2001, p. 71). Because our teachers have completed extensive training and have successfully applied this training, I believe most will change their core teaching practices and, as a result, student-learning practices will change as well (Cuban, 2001, p. 93). I do agree with Cuban when he says that social, political, and organizational changes must occur. Our books and book adoption schedules must change. We must also have proactive administrators who are willing to budget more money to fund unstructured planning time for teachers.

If we do not change, our younger students will continue to demand more of their educational environment. If we can successfully implement change in the earlier grades, the middle schools and high schools will be under pressure to change as well. Some of that is happening now. Our high dropout rate is a signal that we have a problem, and technology might be able to help us solve it. Our Advanced Placement students frequently indicate that they are not sufficiently challenged. One reason could be that they have technology skills, but their teachers are not encouraging them to use these skills. If our teachers can be trained and encouraged to create challenging technology-rich learning environments, we will meet the demands of younger students who want more from their schools. If we don't do this in individual schools, we might see a surge of virtual high schools, similar to those that have recently been established in Louisiana. Such schools cause educators to rely more on distance learning through departments created by state education agencies. A change of this type could reduce the number of teaching positions, which, in turn, could encourage better performance at the local school level.

A major obstacle to creating a better learning environment is that teachers do not have enough unstructured planning time. At work, teachers simply do not have time for even a ninety-minute planning period. The myriad of demands, including grading papers, dealing with dress code infractions, enforcing campus rules, and preparing special education reports, leave little time for learning about technology. Our on-site professional development programs have worked well, but they are not without cost. Teachers who have substitutes taking care of their classes while they are in training go back to mounds of accumulated paperwork, which means they have little time to reflect on the creative ideas that arose during their training. Teachers should not have to incur an extra workload every time they take a training class.

In the past, we used desktop computers housed in makeshift computer labs for our technology integration. This technology was welcomed, but all the electrical cords, cable, wires, and peripherals created problems. Our computer lab resembled a pile of spaghetti! The wireless computers we have purchased with grant monies have eliminated many of these problems. Time is no longer wasted taking students to and from the lab. Now students can work in familiar surroundings with other classroom resources readily available during project work. Our teachers have commented that with laptops, they have more visual control over the class than they do with desktops. Students are more excited about their learning when the lab comes to them. Teachers are more likely to continue using the wireless computers because of their simplicity, comfort, and reliability. Now that we have our teachers excited about using wireless laptops, we need to help them make better use of the desktop lab as well.

Another problem is that most classrooms do not have ready access to technology and must schedule or reserve equipment. Until this situation improves, teachers will find it difficult to significantly alter the way they teach. Teachers often find unexpected uses for technology in the course of the teaching day, and they are frustrated when the equipment is not readily available. Classrooms are much like small individual businesses. We ask teachers to be the owners of that business and to use technology seamlessly even though it is not available all the time. That is much like asking someone to open a business where the telephone is essential to its operation, yet the business manager is required to get in his car and drive to the phone booth at the end of the road. It is equally ridiculous to ask more of teachers without providing them with the necessary tools. We must bring real-world learning to a teacher's real world, the classroom. It is easy to understand why teachers who are isolated in their own classrooms can be drawn to, or shy away from, using technology. Using technology largely depends on the drive and initiative of the teacher even when the tools are available and functioning properly. Again, as Cuban notes in his book, it was the maverick computer-using teachers who made the most profound changes over time (2001, p. 170). We have teachers in our school who would like to be able to use technology as freely as pencil, paper, and books.

It has also been a challenge to customize our training program. In our particular case, it was critical that we had some flexibility in doing so. I have done a significant amount of research on technology programs in the United States, Canada, and Australia. By applying principles learned from those studies, we have taken ownership of our pilot program; we set our own benchmarks and are successfully meeting them. As Cuban notes, it is important that teachers have a say in what works best for them.

In my opinion, the fact that we have a local teacher as technology coach is a strong factor in ensuring the success of our staff development program. Our teachers have responded better to this program than they have to the expensive piped-in training we have tried in the past. My experiences have been classroom-tested in our own school. My wisdom in using technology in education has been derived from trial and error during my twenty-five years as a business teacher. The teachers involved in the learning process have confidence in me, and we have developed a trusting relationship.

To transform our teaching staff, I felt I needed to know our staff well enough to bring out the best in them. To do that, I had to show personal trustworthiness by a clear demonstration of character and competence. Character includes many factors, but it must include a passion to assist teachers no matter what their technology skill level. Competence includes an ability to carry out all the tasks required of the teacher, as well as the desire to learn about new areas the teachers want to explore. My work with teachers does not begin with technology but rather with instructional design and knowledge of how technology fits into that design. I emphasize the interplay of curriculum goals, assessment, the needs of the specific group of learners, instructional strategies, and the value of integrating technology into the curriculum. Because our program is tailor-made, our teachers have accepted it more readily than they would have accepted a mandated state requirement.

I disagree with Cuban when he says that at the high school level, the software applications such as spreadsheets and databases were designed for professionals and should not be used in the classroom (2001, p. 166). We have found, and continue to find, many ways to integrate the Microsoft Office suite into student-centered learning projects. My own teaching has improved because I can use productivity software to strengthen many components of the curriculum.

We have special challenges in teaching high school students because most of them have had years of exposure to technology in their homes. In our case, I disagree with Cuban's findings that the majority of teachers frequently use computers at home, particularly for school purposes (2001, p. 83). Students today have had the time to experiment with technology at home, whereas parents and teachers have not. Students have learned a great deal about technology from "incidental learning" or learning accompanied by discovery. Routinely, parents and teachers have adult responsibilities that simply do not allow that to happen. Students in high school know a great deal about technology, but they do not know how to productively use business software to solve real-world problems. Adults in the work world have that knowledge, but teachers do not. This is where our teachers need to catch up in their training so they will be able to lead by example, using software that is used in the real world for real-world learning.

Only if time is set aside specifically for staff development can we put those issues to rest. Most teachers have little time to learn the needed skills at home. For a significant change to occur, I believe training must be provided at school in cooperative groups. This will require organizational changes.

If our school adopts the proposed schedule of nine weeks on followed by two weeks off, I suggest that we offer paid staff development during the two-week period between academic sessions. This would eliminate many of the scheduling and organizational problems that we are experiencing now and would allow us to revisit individual training goals. Cuban mentions in his book that this can be a significant barrier to progress. He calls the process for change the "slow revolution" and discusses structural barriers that need to be overcome in the school setting (2001, p. 170).

CONCLUSION

I don't think Cuban is promoting the idea that all our efforts to promote technology have been to no avail. I believe he wants us to approach our process of teaching in a way that makes a difference we have not yet seen. I want to see organizational changes in our schools that will allow teachers to make a difference. I know Cuban is not against using computers in our schools; he is just raising the issue that we should look at the problem in a more logical and constructive way. He is giving us food for thought that is causing us to ask questions. We need the wakeup call. Besides, if by making the structural changes he suggests we encourage more spending, additional technology resources that will make classroom learning more accessible will follow. However, using those resources wisely and productively is always the bottom line.

We need to observe what is happening in classrooms that are successfully integrating technology, learn to reproduce that success in other classrooms, and analyze test scores to justify the costs and changes that will be necessary. Pairing up with Dell, Apple, IBM, and other companies along with being wired up does not mean we are fired up. That's the next step in teacher training. We must now focus on the issues that matter: ready and functioning technology supported by teachers who can lead and a technical staff that can help teachers use technology for student-centered, project-based learning. Data must be collected for longer than one year to determine if we are then "overused and undersold."

To make a difference nationally, we must pay particular attention to the needs and interests of novice teachers, who are often reluctant to use technology. I believe we must make a sustained commitment over three to five years to provide about thirty hours of staff training per year. The emphasis must be on improving basic skills. Cuban seems to agree (2001, p. 179). With that focus, teachers who are reluctant to use technology may be won over, and we will have a greater chance of making a lasting change nationwide.

We have not unleashed the potential to tackle the theory of "oversold and underused," but it is time we began. As Cuban explains, it is too soon to call the investment in computers in schools a failure (2001, p. 187). Much remains to be done. Pressure for schools to integrate technology seamlessly into their curricula may be forced by demand

(Guthrie, 2002). Online and distance learning programs may put high schools and local college programs in direct competition for students. Colleges can often do a better job of integrating technology because their structure is more relaxed and students are generally more focused. If students are allowed to earn high school credit from these institutions, high schools will be forced to make some changes. State departments of education may begin to create virtual high schools to meet the needs of all schools. In any case, changes in structure will have to occur.

One thing is evident: In our school, our ability to customize our professional development program has brought us much closer to achieving our goals. As Cuban notes, schools and teachers can change (2001, p. 195).

REFERENCES

Cuban, Larry. (2001). *Oversold and underused: Computers in the classroom.* Cambridge, MA: Harvard University Press.

Guthrie, James W. (2002). *Instructional technology and educational policy.* Alexandria, VA: CNAC.

9

USING TECHNOLOGY TO ENGAGE STUDENTS FOR MULTIPLE LEARNING EXPERIENCES

Mary Haney and Elaine B. Wilkins

Ida B. Wells Academy, Memphis, Tennessee

Our mission is to provide quality-learning experiences that prepare all students for academic and social success, and to help all students become productive members in a technological and global society.

INTRODUCTION

Resistance to change is part of human behavior; however, transformations in the way we do things in the educational arena—especially in regard to technology—have given some teachers great joy. Whereas some teachers leap at the chance to use new technology, others remain comfortable doing things the way they always have. The attitude of these comfortable teachers is, "Why change it if it isn't broken?" They see themselves as givers of knowledge, and students as receivers. In contrast, Academy teachers are always searching for new and better ways to reach students. We consider ourselves to be facilitators of learning, with students being discoverers of knowledge.

Cuban (2001) states that in the late 1990s, less than 10 percent of teachers used computers in class at least once a week, 20 to 30 percent used computers rarely, and the majority did not use computers at all. Students rarely used computers to create any projects other than research papers. Fewer than 5 percent of teachers regularly used computers in their everyday instruction, and most teachers who used computers did not change their way of teaching.

Two explanations for the underuse of computers in the classroom are given in Cuban (2001). One is that, historically, in both education and business, there has been a lag time between an invention and its use. Small changes accumulating steadily over time have gradually changed the way teachers teach. For example, over time, teachers went from total dependence on chalkboards and textbooks to incorporating overhead projectors and videocassette recorders (VCRs) into their instructional methods. Such slow changes have often occurred over decades rather than over a few months or years.

The second explanation for underuse of computers in the classroom centers on the historical, social, organizational, and political contexts of teaching (Cuban, 2001). Both the corporate sector and public officials believed that new technology would help American schools produce students who were the academic equals of students in foreign countries who were learning the skills needed to compete in the work force. The external influences help to explain why the American public believes that schools that are well equipped with computers have an advantage over those that are not.

BACKGROUND

Ida B. Wells Academy, a Memphis City School, is a Title I at-risk alternative school located in Memphis, Tennessee. We originally provided services for 100 seventh-grade students from across the district each year. The Academy has served more than 500 seventh- and eighth-grade students since its inception in 1995. Presently, seventh- and eighth-grade students may attend the Academy if they are over age and are performing below grade level in reading or mathematics. Students who have been unsuccessful in the traditional school setting, have a high rate of absenteeism or multiple suspensions, or have had numerous conflicts with peers or adults are prime candidates for the Academy. Students are referred to the Academy by their principals, guidance counselors, or parents. Today, the Academy accommodates a maximum of fifty seventh-grade students and fifty eighth-grade students; these students attend the school 200 days a year.

Ida B. Wells Academy has ten teachers. Of these, seven are African American and three are white. Other staff members include the principal, an administrative assistant, one computer technician, an educational assistant, an enrichment facilitator (resource teacher), an in-school suspension specialist, two caseworkers, one school psychologist, and a special projects coordinator.

Because these students experienced minimal success in the traditional classroom, Academy teachers use alternative instructional and assessment methods. The teachers also incorporate Howard Gardner's theory of multiple intelligences in curriculum development, daily instruction, and assessment (Dobbs, 2001). According to Dobbs, results of a Multiple Intelligences Survey administered to students at the beginning of each year indicate that a majority of students at the academy are visual/spatial (like to draw), interpersonal (like to talk), and bodily/kinesthetic (like to move). The students learn best through activities that incorporate these three intelligences; therefore, cooperative group activities, integrated thematic units, and hands-on projects are strategies that have been used effectively in classrooms at the Academy.

Because at-risk students often do not trust or get along with others in a group, cooperative group activities sometimes do not work well. Likewise, integrated thematic units sometimes do not work well for the at-risk alternative school student population. Because of chronic absenteeism, students sometimes have not developed the research skills needed to complete activities. However, unlike traditional research methods that limit students to printed media above their reading level, Internet research offers material on a wide variety of reading levels.

When they assigned traditional hands-on projects, teachers at the Academy found that students did not bring the materials they needed to complete projects. When supplied with materials, students did not claim ownership of the projects and did not create quality work. On the other hand, when they use computers to complete curricular activities, most students create quality work of which they are proud. Computers, for example, provide ways for visual/spatial, bodily/kinesthetic, and interpersonal learners to participate in activities, explorations, and investigations they would not otherwise experience.

The Southern Association of Colleges and Schools (SACS) Study (Davis & Stewart, 2001) for Ida B. Wells Academy reflects the following staff beliefs about teaching and learning:

- Student success is the chief priority in the Ida B. Wells Academy learning community.
- All students can learn at higher levels.
- Students learn in different ways and should be provided with a variety of instructional approaches to support their learning.
- Students should not only be able to demonstrate their understanding of essential knowledge and skills but also be actively involved in solving problems and producing quality work.
- Our school should promote learning opportunities for all stakeholders.

Because of these beliefs, we think student achievement will increase through the use of real-world tasks and authentic performance activities provided via technology. The vision of Ida B. Wells Academy is to be a nurturing, caring, cooperative learning community in which all stakeholders (students, parents, staff, and community representatives) experience daily success. In this learning environment, all students have equal access and varied opportunities to develop their intelligences, while learning to become productive in society. The vision (Davis & Stewart, 2001), which is a description of desired results for student learning at the Academy, focuses on the following goals:

- Expanding and integrating knowledge:
  - Students see school life as continuous improvement and preparation for life.
  - Students use prior knowledge and skills to create original products and performances in new situations.
- Thinking and reasoning skills:
  - Students evaluate, analyze, and infer information to solve real-world problems.
  - Students apply problem-solving strategies to address all issues they encounter.

- Assuming personal and social responsibility:
  - Students accept responsibility for the choices they make.
  - Students critically process situations and make appropriate choices in resolving conflicts.

TENNESSEE STATE BOARD OF EDUCATION STRATEGIC PLAN, 2000

The *Master Plan for Tennessee Schools Preparing for the 21st Century* (State Board of Education, 2002) contains a goal for using technology to improve student learning and meet specific performance goals. School districts are required to:

- Focus technology resources to improve student learning.
- Provide all students with access to networked computers in the classroom.
- Use technology to advance student learning and ensure that all students are prepared for high-skilled, high-wage jobs and to support lifelong learning.
- Increase the development and use of Web-based resources.
- [Provide] . . . opportunities for teachers and administrators to develop competence in using technology to meet instructional goals.
- Obtain or develop on-line instruction to meet individual student and teacher learning needs and course requirements.

TECHNOLOGY INFUSION AT IDA B. WELLS ACADEMY

At Ida B. Wells Academy, teachers make an effort not just to add technology to the curriculum but also to infuse technology into the curriculum. Technology is both subject matter and delivery method for learning that is engaging, interactive, encouraging, and long lasting. The Academy teachers are attempting to use the Memphis City Schools curriculum standards and to fully incorporate technology into everyday learning. The Academy's ultimate goal is to ensure that students can access, assimilate, apply, and adapt to existing and emerging technologies as lifelong learners in a global community. The staff aligned the following Memphis City Schools goals for technology improvement with technology goals at the Academy:

- To create a challenging, supportive educational environment that results in higher levels of achievement for all students.
- To help all staff become educational leaders responsible for providing quality leadership at all levels to achieve quality instruction for students.
- To hold everyone at the Academy accountable for contributing to the educational bottom line, which is student achievement.

As a part of its Technology Literacy Challenge Fund (TLCF) grant, the Ida B. Wells Academy staff created benchmarks (http://www.ibwa-edu. org/benchmarks/bm.html) to measure improvement in the areas of curriculum, instruction, and organization. The benchmarks comprise three phases, with specific indicators and evidence for each phase. Each indicator in the three phases represents a progression toward attaining the benchmark. The evidence for each phase includes items such as documentation of teacher training, lesson plans, projects and products, weekly logs, and observations.

The curriculum benchmark states that technology is aligned with the standards-based curriculum of the Memphis City Schools and the state of Tennessee and that technology is infused in all content areas. Benchmarks for instruction state that teaching strategies reflect the incorporation of current best practices of technology-supported learning; that teachers plan lessons infusing technology to support the Memphis City Schools curriculum maps, Memphis City Schools standards, and state standards; and that teachers provide current technology training and support for students. The organization benchmarks state that (1) the technology coach provides technology training and support for individual teachers, small groups of teachers, and the entire faculty on basic computer operations and concepts, setup and maintenance, and telecommunications; (2) individual teachers, small groups of teachers, and the entire teaching staff attend local, state, or national professional development activities to gain knowledge about software and productivity tools; and (3) a full-time technology coach is responsible for training, scheduling, and support for teachers, as well as for TLCF compliance.

The Ida B. Wells Academy School Improvement Plan (2001) includes strategies and activities for technology integration in each subject area. For language arts, the strategy is to develop alternative methods of assessment using technology. Computers are to be used for focused instruction with the pre-algebra curriculum. The science strategy is to use the Internet and reference software to complete research and lab simulations. In social studies, the strategy is to provide a variety of educational software to supplement and complement concepts, information, and social studies skills. Teachers are also expected to use the World Wide Web in the classroom to conduct research and create simulations and educational software for word processing.

Instruction—Past, Present, and Future

Howard Gardner's theory of multiple intelligences is the foundation for the Ida B. Wells Academy curriculum (Dobbs, 2001). According to Gardner, intelligence comprises at least eight distinct abilities that work either separately or together. Each person has his or her own blend of intelligences—his or her own way of learning. The eight intelligences Gardner identifies are interpersonal, intrapersonal, verbal/linguistic, visual/spatial, logical/mathematical, bodily/kinesthetic, musical/rhythmic, and naturalist.

Initially, instruction at the Academy was delivered primarily through lecture and demonstration. Paper and pencil drill and practice activities were often assigned. Because students at the Academy had experienced little success in the traditional textbook-oriented classroom, and most were two or more years below grade level academically, textbooks were used mainly for resource or reference materials. Students worked in cooperative groups to complete hands-on activities, as well as projects that resulted in paper-and-pencil products. Computers were used mainly in the science computer lab, where students did research using a multimedia encyclopedia and typed their research papers.

Many classrooms had only a teacher workstation with a presentation monitor, or a small number of computers. Where there were one or more computers, the teacher workstation was used to demonstrate directions, concepts, and applications. Sometimes, students worked in cooperative groups in which one or more students would be working at the computer while the others worked on hands-on components of the projects. Students would then use the teacher workstation and presentation monitor to present projects. In other situations, the teacher workstation was used as an electronic chalkboard. Students would all answer a question or solve a problem, either individually or in teams. A third use for the teacher workstation would be to present a warm-up activity for all students to complete at their desks. The teacher workstation and presentation station could be used to view online programs that the whole class participated in or discussed (for example, http://www.brainpop.com).

With the TLCF 2001 grant, each core subject teacher acquired ten computers for classroom use. As a result, instruction has changed considerably. Teachers are becoming facilitators, rather than lecturers. They are planning lessons in which technology is the major tool for instruction and learning. In their lessons, teachers are using the Internet for WebQuests, think quests, scavenger hunts, research, lesson introductions, and real-time views from space. Lessons involve locating examples of music from specific composers or genres, viewing art at online museums, and taking online quizzes.

Use of the computer has allowed students to become active researchers, a strategy that makes research more learner-centered and less teacher-directed. Students with diverse intelligences collaborate to complete projects. Students research, experience virtual field trips, complete interactive activities online, and locate information and graphics needed for the resulting research-based multimedia presentations. For most teachers, paper-and-pencil drill-and-practice activities have primarily been relegated to homework.

In the future, Academy teachers should be able to plan online mini-units and long-term projects. Projects should integrate the different curricula. The projects should incorporate interactive activities, lesson links, Internet research, rubrics, and collaborative projects with other schools. Assessment should include online quizzes, for which a final multimedia product will be required. Students should be able to use Microsoft Office products to create interactive reviews for use by other students both in school and online.

Computers—Past, Present, and Future

When Ida B. Wells Academy opened in 1995, the two computers available were located in the office and were used for administrative purposes. In early 1996, one science teacher received ten new, outdated MacIntosh computers for a science computer lab; the computers were not networked. The school invested in a classroom telephone line that would allow the science computer lab to access an Internet service provider (ISP). The telephone line was shared with the language arts class adjacent to the science computer lab. A second telephone line was installed in a mathematics classroom, thus giving this classroom Internet accessibility as well. At the time, other teachers at the Academy expressed no interest in using technology in the classroom, although most did want to have a computer "on the desk." With the ISP, only one computer in each of the classrooms could access the Internet; a modem was used to obtain Internet access.

There was also a networked Computer Curriculum Corporation (CCC)/Pearson Education (NCS Learn) computer lab used for remedial mathematics, language arts, and reading. This lab, which had no Internet connections, was dismantled in the fall of 2001 when the computer technician was transferred to another school. In November 2001, the Scholastic Read 180 program for struggling readers was implemented in the language arts curriculum. Two components of the NCS Learn (CCC) program (Mathematics Investigations and Mathematics Concepts and Skills) will be implemented in the mathematics curriculum immediately on receipt of the program materials.

In 1996, the Academy staff developed an informal long-range school technology acquisition plan designed to enhance instruction in the classroom via technology. According to the plan, each year one discipline would get four classroom computers purchased with district funds. Two computers were obtained for a media center through library services. Three additional computers and a teacher workstation were obtained with Goals 2000 grant monies. By the end of 2000, each classroom had at least two computers purchased with district funds. Two teachers were each awarded a Rotary Teacher Initiative Grant to buy a digital camera for their classrooms.

The school technology acquisition plan was implemented in 1997 when the school purchased four IBM computers for the mathematics classroom. The mathematics teacher wanted her classes to be proficient with the use of IBM compatible computers. In addition, the teacher asked for and received donated computers from businesses and from the State Department of Education (ancient '286, '386, and '486 computers, with a top speed of 66 MHz). The donated computers had DOS and Windows 3.1 only, so the computers would not run up-to-date math programs. However, the computers would run shareware and freeware drill-and-practice activities. The donated computers were also used in one language arts classroom for word processing.

In the early years of the Academy, one science teacher, one math teacher, and one language arts teacher used computers in the classrooms. These three teachers brought equipment such as computers, scanners, and printers from home. They also purchased programs and peripheral equipment, such as switch boxes, printer cables, mice, and ZIP drives to provide limited access to technology for their students.

Each year subsequent to the development of the school technology acquisition plan, two computers were purchased for each teacher in a specific discipline. Teachers who had a presentation station used the station for whole-group instruction, or students took turns completing computer assignments in cooperative groups. However, students were unable to explore the programs on topics such as body systems and weather individually.

In 2001, there have been major equipment enhancements at Ida B. Wells Academy as a result of the TLCF grant. Mathematics and reading remediation needs will be addressed in the classroom, and the NCS Learn mathematics program will be available for seventh- and eighth-grade students. A Goals 2000 grant provided computers, support, a Scholastic Read 180 software program, and Scholastic books to increase the student reading levels of seventh- and eighth-grade students. The Read 180 program has been implemented in language arts classrooms. The Goals 2000 grant program is used with all students during the regular class day, as well as with selected students before and after school.

Each core subject classroom has ten networked computers, and each music and art class has six computers with up-to-date operating system software and Microsoft Office XP. All classrooms have networked Internet access, a networked laser printer, a color inkjet printer, a digital camera, and a scanner, as well as a presentation monitor. In addition, the school has a color laser printer and a Sony projector for presentations. A parent, teacher, and community resource room houses four Internet-connected computers, a laser printer, and a color copier for adults in the Ida B. Wells Academy learning community. Obviously, the Academy has a wealth of hardware. Teachers have discovered, however, that fewer computers would suffice because much of their planned instruction involves using small groups that rotate to learning stations.

The plan is to replace outdated computers each year according to the schedule outlined in the school technology acquisition plan. The Memphis City Schools district will no longer provide service for outdated computers, so computers that cannot accommodate modern software will be worthless.

Teacher Use of Computers—Past, Present, and Future

When the Academy opened, a few teachers had a computer at home for typing lesson plans, managing grades, and typing tests. As teachers acquired classroom computers, they used the computers for drill and practice, some research using multimedia encyclopedias, and word processing. The dinosaur laptops donated to the Academy by the State Department of Education allowed some teachers to use a grade book program and type their lesson plans.

One of the TLCF grant goals is for teachers to infuse technology into the curriculum to improve student achievement in all subject areas on the Tennessee Comprehensive Assessment Program (TCAP), the TCAP Writing Assessment, and the Iowa Tests of Basic Skills. To meet this goal, all teachers are trying to use technology tools and productivity tools (e.g., Microsoft Office) to enhance and support student projects. Students use Microsoft Office to create fliers, poetry, posters, booklets, letters, reports, graphs, and charts.

Teachers have become more dependent on the computer for daily classroom tasks. They use the computer to report daily attendance, check for messages about in-school or district meetings, submit weekly lesson plans, and manage their grades. Teachers are excited about their ability to use the computer for both instructional tasks and student assessment, but they want detailed written instructions for all technology procedures, such as how to upload images from the camera and how to use the scanner.

Teachers are beginning to think more about technology infusion when planning instructional activities. As they look at the standards and curriculum maps, teachers are beginning to think of more than one way to infuse technology into a lesson and to conduct a more in-depth study of a concept. Teachers are also using what they've learned about technology to do projects for college classes they attend, as well as for home management.

In the future, teachers will be expected to be proficient with Microsoft Office programs and with use of the Internet, computer, printer, scanner, and digital camera. Teachers should also be using technology daily in their teaching and automatically thinking of ways to use the computer to teach any topic or concept.

Student Use of Computers—Past, Present, and Future

The first use of computers at Ida B. Wells Academy was in the CCC lab and the science computer lab. Structured remediation drill-and-practice activities in language arts, reading, and mathematics were provided in the CCC lab. In the science lab, students used computers for research in multimedia encyclopedias and typed reports using information they had located. They viewed science software and Internet activities on the presentation station, sometimes working in cooperative groups, but they had little chance to complete individual work. Once the math computers were installed, students could complete individual drill-and-practice exercises. Students also used the outdated computers in the language arts classrooms for word processing of poetry, short stories, and reports. Some students used computers to create and design cards, banners, posters, and seasonal coloring books, which were delivered to local children's hospitals, area nursing homes and adopters, and daycare centers. Others learned to repair and refurbish older computers, including learning the DOS commands needed to install and run programs.

Today, students at the Academy use computers every day. They are active researchers on the Internet, and the research conducted is more learner-centered and less teacher-directed. Students with diverse intelligence needs collaborate to complete projects. In addition, students create Web pages for communication, experience virtual field trips, complete interactive activities online, and locate information and graphics for research-based presentations. They analyze classroom data (grades, conduct, and attendance) and create graphs, charts, and spreadsheets to compare their average to the class average. All students have created more than one Microsoft PowerPoint presentation in which they incorporated what they typed in Microsoft Word, graphs they created in Microsoft Excel, and pictures or images from the Internet or clip art files.

Today, students view the computer as more than just a "game machine." They are proud of their work on the computer and love to show off their products. Most students want to incorporate the computers into all classroom activities, and state that they prefer to edit essays on the computer because rewrites are unnecessary. Students demonstrate computer knowledge and skill by helping each other and the teachers. Some students who, in the past, have not performed well academically have become technology leaders in the classroom. Grades are improving because students enthusiastically complete classroom assignments that require use of technology. Examples of technology-oriented student work are exhibited on bulletin boards inside classrooms, on doors, and throughout the halls.

In the future, all Academy students will be expected to use technology in everyday learning activities. Like teachers, students will be expected to become proficient with Microsoft Office software, as well as using the Internet, computers, printers, scanners, and digital cameras. Computers will be used for project-based activities that require use of problem-solving skills. Students will create expressive Web pages, think quests, WebQuests, and scavenger hunts. They will also review activities for electronic publication. Technology service learning activities (in student technology teams) will provide real-world opportunities for Academy students to use their technology skills. The district no longer allows service-learning activities, but these activities have considerable social, civic, and academic value, and we hope they will be re-incorporated into the curriculum. Students who show an aptitude for computer technology will also be trained to be "student techs" so that they can troubleshoot problems in the classrooms.

Technology Professional Development

Before Ida B. Wells Academy opened, a few teachers had attended state and local technology conferences. Some teachers had taught themselves how to use the productivity tools they had purchased for home use. The more technologically proficient teachers at the Academy taught some of their colleagues to use certain software programs, and some teachers attended local computer workshops presented by the Memphis City School district, as well as courses given at local universities. However, the workshops covered too much material in too little time, and there was no support for teachers after they returned to the Academy. Without access to needed hardware and software, teachers were unable to use their new knowledge and did not retain it. Consequently, some teachers lost their interest in learning technology skills.

The TLCF grant gave teachers the opportunity to learn new strategies for using technology to transform teaching and learning. Teachers, staff, and parents can attend Saturday workshops on how to use the Internet and productivity tools such as Word, Excel, and PowerPoint. At weekly faculty meetings, the technology coach and other staff present mini-workshops called "Technology Bytes." Teachers have practice time immediately after the workshops. The technology coach offers local after-school workshops and will provide individual training for teachers during their planning time. Teachers have also attended after-school and full-day workshops at the Teaching and Learning Academy. All teachers attended the Memphis City Schools Technology Conference, and some attended the Tennessee Educational Technology Conference in Nashville and conferences in Memphis presented by Microsoft. In the future, teachers will be expected to be presenters at local, state, and national technology conferences.

For two weeks in spring 2002, the Ida B. Wells Academy staff provided technology professional development for other teachers in the Memphis City School District. As Academy teachers shared knowledge and skills, their knowledge and skills were reinforced.

The technology coach, with the assistance of Academy teachers, presents monthly technology mini-workshops for parents. In summer 2002, the Academy hosted a technology fair for area parents, teachers, adopters, and the community.

The Ida B. Wells Academy Home Page
(http://www.ibwa-edu.org)

The Ida B. Wells Academy Web master, who was self-taught, created the school Web page in January 1997. The Web page was used mainly to communicate information about the school and to display outstanding student work and achievements. The Web page evolved to showcase many school programs and student activities, with links being added to assist teachers; however, the site was not being used to full advantage.

The school Web page has changed considerably. Today, the Academy Web page is more than a static page listing school information such as the mission, vision, belief statements, school calendar, and memories of past activities. Now parents can find a calendar of parent meetings, links to parent sites, and a parent multiple-intelligences survey. People throughout the world can link to the school website and obtain information about the TLCF grant and benchmarks, weekly reflective journals, and technology best practices developed by Academy teachers.

A section called "Teacher Stuff" was created to facilitate time management and eliminate paperwork. "Teacher Stuff" includes curriculum maps, professional development resources, lesson plan data and a lesson plan generator, state Tennessee Comprehensive Assessment Program data, workshops presented at the Academy, technology work orders, and various forms that can be completed online and submitted to the principal or appropriate others.

In the future, the Academy Web page will include teacher-created classroom Web pages where students and parents can obtain information about homework and the six-week syllabus, check students' grades online, view class pictures, and keep abreast of student honors and awards. In the future, student-created Web pages will showcase products from class assignments, field trip reports, and art and literary compositions. Parents and others in the community will create Web page links that highlight calendars of area and adopter activities.

CONCLUSION

Today, the public expects measurable results from public schools. Appropriate and innovative use of technology is essential for improving performance. When used effectively, technology enhances how teachers teach and students learn. During the last decade, the focus was on broad dissemination of the technology and the teaching of basic literacy to the population at large. Now we can begin to explore new approaches that will allow us to enhance learning in measurable ways.

The Academy staff agrees that in most schools computers are underused. We believe that change does take time, but our teachers are making the effort to change the way they teach and the way students learn. The TLCF grant had a major impact on the use of technology in our school. We now have the most up-to-date computers, peripherals, and software. All computers are networked and have Internet access. Most important, we offer continuous professional development and support for the training provided.

Students at Ida B. Wells Academy have become consumers of knowledge and information. They have become discoverers of knowledge rather than receivers of information presented by the teacher. Technology has become a major instructional tool at the Academy. We believe that the technology program and practices established at Ida B. Wells Academy can enhance student learning not only in an at-risk alternative school setting but in a traditional school as well. Even though our new equipment has been in place only a few months, we plan to analyze TCAP data at the end of the year to see if the use of technology has had an impact on student achievement. We will be in a better position to measure the impact of technology infusion at the end of the 2002–2003 school year, after our seventh-grade students have had a full year to use the technology.

Technology alone cannot make the needed difference; support is necessary as well. Administrators must set an example by supporting the use of computers in the classroom. Opportunities for professional development are necessary, both during and after school hours, as well as on Saturdays; comp time or monetary incentives encourage teachers to become involved in after-hours training. A technology coach is on campus daily to help teachers increase their skills. No matter what their skill level, all teachers are involved in the use of technology as a teaching tool in the classroom; each is becoming a capable facilitator in the technology-infusion experiences at the Academy.

REFERENCES

Cuban, L. (2001). *Oversold and Underused: Computers in the Classroom.* Harvard University Press, Cambridge, MA.

Davis, S. & Stewart, M. (2001). Ida B. Wells Academy Southern Association of Colleges and Schools (SACS) Study (unpublished).

Dobbs, V. R. (2001). *The relationship between implementation of the multiple intelligences theory in the curriculum and student academic achievement at a seventh grade at-risk alternative school.* Nashville. Southern Bindery.

Ida B. Wells Academy School Improvement Plan (SIP). (2001, unpublished).

Standards for Alternative Schools, at http://www.state.tn.us/sbe/aternativeschool.htm.

State Board of Education (2002). *Master Plan for Tennessee Schools Preparing for the 21st Century,* at http://www.state.tn.us/sbe/master.htm.

AFTERWORD

Laurence Peters
*Director Mid-Atlantic Regional Technology
in Education Consortium (MAR*TEC)*

In the Hans Christian Andersen fairy story "The Emperor's New Clothes," it is the boy in the crowd who shrieks that the emperor is naked—and in one fell swoop the reign of politically corrected vision is over. It remains for most of us an unforgettable moment in our childhood when we first experience the liberating power of laughter breaking through layers of adult hypocrisy and fear. Without doubt, there is some of that same refreshing icon-busting emotion contained in Cuban's book: Technology has been oversold and underused—even in schools located at the heart of the digital revolution in Silicon Valley! But where do we go from here? Clearly, it is not Cuban's intention to suggest that the reason the technology was "oversold and underused" is that it lacks intrinsic educational value, rather his goal is to raise hard questions for those outside the classroom—policymakers in particular, who have been so enamored of all things technological that they have ignored the weight of existing practice that teachers must continue to carry around despite the distractions of having high-tech machines in their classrooms. So clearly, a major conclusion to be drawn from Cuban's analysis and confirmed by these writers is that the "heavy lifting" of making the investment in technology work cannot be completed by teachers situated in traditional work roles who are isolated from each other, as well as from technical and intellectual support. Second, there is no one solution that can be replicated for all schools and districts; rather than roadmaps, we have trailways—paths that some have begun to tread but are recorded on few, if any, maps. To turn these trailways into roads, we need a more robust system for capturing the variety of ways in which schools are approaching the challenge and reporting results to the community, a community that is still hesitant to leave the safety zones that enable technology and curriculum to exist in two separate and barely overlapping worlds. Even the research that Larry Cuban conducted for his study was based on only a seven months' survey of two high-tech schools located in Silicon Valley. Moreover, it was done without any reference to student achievement or analysis of how the time spent by the so-called heavy users of technology differed from the less-dependent users and what difference that made to the student outcomes.

A further value of these essays is to serve as a corrective to Cuban's tendency to see technology in blanket terms, as if the use of computers in classrooms did not differ in significant ways from the uses of educational television or slide projectors. Although this is not an uncommon view, the danger is that researchers can be all too easily captured by it. These essays encourage a more nuanced view of technology investments, one that nurtures a more complex decision-making environment than one that simply suggests that we must have more of whatever quantity of new and exciting machines and software the ever-present vendors are knocking on the door to sell. The writers collected here help us to engage more thoughtfully in the ongoing conversation that Larry Cuban began with his book, a conversation that can essentially be boiled down to the simple question: So now that we have the new machines, so what? Four themes or "lessons learned" might be identified from these essays that suggest some ways that technology can become a more valued part of the curriculum rather than some type of luxury that is seen as secondary to the school's mission:

1. *Technology can never be justified for its own sake but must be defined against a set of learning goals.* Starting with the learning goal instead of focusing on the tremendous capacities of the latest generation of software, the right question to ask is, how can student learning can be supported by technology? The situation should not

be the other way around, where teachers are meant to experiment with how technology can support what they are already doing. One way to stimulate such a discussion is for school districts to set an ambitious goal such as the need to reach all students. The next step might be to determine how teachers can best use technology to reach those students that all agree are the hardest to reach, whether they are labeled as learning disabled or not. Thomas Pfundstein says it best when he describes how his own Cleveland school district has incorporated within its technology plan the goal that its investment will be used to "create lifelong learning opportunities for all segments of the community." Such a concept would have been unheard of a decade ago, but now, with innovative Internet-based software such as Blackboard.com available, that goal could become a reality—as can the promise of meeting the individual learning style needs of an increasingly diverse range of learners. In his account, Pfundstein makes concrete the simple ways in which a variety of students can benefit—from the deaf student who no longer needs a translator because he can use e-mail to communicate with his teacher to the ESL student who no longer needs an oral translator because she can read the classroom notes on a website.

2. *The conversation about technology must be firmly harnessed to the raising of student achievement; if technology is going to continue to deserve the budgets that it has previously enjoyed, it will increasingly have to respond to what difference it makes in the classroom.* A question that is seldom raised is, given that there are a finite number of hours in a school day, what traditional tasks will the technology-based activities replace? What are the things that technology can do better than traditional instruction, and for what types of students? This is not a trivial or academic question; it is the basis of the fear expressed by Diane Bennett when she worries that her Advanced Placement students will desert her school for a virtual high school where their sophisticated technology skills can find more challenging outlets.

3. *We need a variety of approaches to professional development, not a "one-size fits all," cookie cutter approach.* Every profession nowadays faces the challenge of mastering new technologies, whether it is lawyers, bankers, or physicians. The professional development (as

is the technical support necessary to maintain it in functional order) is typically considered not as an afterthought but is designed and managed before a piece of equipment is purchased. By contrast, teachers have had to make it up as they went along, and the results of this ad hoc way of doing things are currently evident in schools in Silicon Valley and beyond. What seems to be emerging from these essays, reflecting current practice, is the development of a mix of incentives and opportunities that combine "just in time" assistance with opportunities to practice skills after work hours. Although Ida B. Wells Academy (as described by Mary Haney and Elaine Wilkins) is probably an exception in that it offers the assistance of a technology coach along with many professional development opportunities, the spirit of providing some redundancy in choices and flexible arrangements is certainly a trend that will need to continue if we are to break out of the Cuban rap that technology is "oversold and underused."

4. *These writers also remind us that if we are to overcome the type of obstacles to successful integration of technology that Cuban has identified, we must draw on the collective talents of teachers.* To be successful, such a plan requires sustained leadership, as is exhibited in the case studies represented here. Some have taken a historical view of their role. For example, in describing her school district in Doddridge County, Christine Richards quotes futurist Robert Tinker: "We are helping write the script of the opening scenes of the most dramatic play educators have ever witnessed. Our grandchildren will write the final scene, and their children will enjoy its impact." Blake West uses the analogy of a partially built bridge, saying that even though the bridge stretches only part of the way across the river, a few teachers "decide to take their children to the brink, jump in, and swim the rest of the way to the shore." Whether it is we or our grandchildren who either swim or cross the bridge to that distant shore, the struggles recorded here are exciting and inspiring. They inspire us not to give up the journey but to attack the challenges with new hope and confidence.

Policymakers looking to break out of the simplistic sound bites that have led to an era in which technology has been oversold and underused might do well to reflect on these essays and talk about the need for more balanced approaches, ones that enable the kind of gifted leadership represented in these essays to have more control over the budgetary decisions affecting technology spending, so that, for example, well-functioning libraries are not turned into media rooms with computers favored over books, and professional development is not cut because it does not help to increase the computer-student ratio.

The persuasive power of these essays for policymakers and others is that they cannot be criticized as the product of armchair theorists: They were written by those who live and breathe the daily classroom realities that often escape those who are in typical leadership positions. The authors have had to forge their own visions of how to move their schools, colleges, and districts forward, and in so doing they have often had to ask difficult questions and sometimes receive back some discomforting answers. Bell and Wilson from the Curry School of Education reveal, for example, that that only six of the fourteen preservice teachers in their science education program managed to use technology to "transform the science curriculum." But they draw strength from the fact that this was achieved despite issues of insufficient computers and a lack of receptive school culture. They also wisely conclude that the returns on that investment can be considerable and the "success of a single technologically innovative teacher has the potential to influence the practice of other open-minded and committed teachers in the school." Indeed, a modest expectation for this book is that it will do something of the same—that it will quietly influence the larger conversation that must continue and encourage other teachers and school leaders to forge ahead knowing they are not quite so isolated as they once thought.

INDEX

ABOUT THE CONTRIBUTORS

Randy L. Bell formerly taught middle and high school science in a rural community in eastern Oregon. Since earning his Ph.D. in science education from Oregon State University, his research has focused on teaching the nature of science and on technology infusion in science instruction. Dr. Bell is an assistant professor of science education in the Curry School of Education at the University of Virginia, where he teaches courses in secondary science methods, educational technology, and science education research methods. His primary research interests are teaching and learning about the nature of science and scientific inquiry.

Diane Bennett is currently the technology coach for Mt. Juliet High School in Mt. Juliet, Tennessee. She and her colleagues are implementing a model program that is supported by a Technology Literacy Challenge Fund grant. The grant is funded through Tennessee's State Department of Education for $200,000. Diane has twenty-five years of teaching experience at Mt. Juliet High School in business and vocational education, with primary responsibility for teaching computer technology to students in grades 10 through 12.

Larry Cuban is the author of *Oversold and Underused: Computers in the Classroom*, which is published by Harvard University Press. This book probes several public schools in or near Silicon Valley in California. Dr. Cuban is professor emeritus of education at Stanford University. Between 1981 and 2001, students in the School of Education voted him "Teacher of the Year" seven times. He was the Arlington County, Virginia, school superintendent for seven years, and previously spent fourteen years teaching social studies in inner city high schools. In addition to his recent book on school use of educational technology, he has also written *Reconstructing the Common Good in Education* (co-edited with Dorothy Shipps, 2000); "Managing the Dilemmas of High School Reform" in *Curriculum Inquiry* (2000); *How Scholars Trumped Teachers: Change without Reform in University Curriculum, Teaching, and Research*, 1890–1990 (1999); and *Tinkering Toward Utopia: Reflections on School Reform* (with David Tyack, 1995).

James E. Eschenmann is the technology coordinator for the Harrison County Board of Education in West Virginia, a position he has held since 1996. He has a wealth of experience as leader, project coordinator, and teacher at all levels of education. He is currently overseeing the development and implementation of a broadband wide area network to connect all schools within Harrison County. He continues to serve as the chairman of the Harrison County Technology Committee. In 1995, he received the Technology and Learning Teacher of the Year award for West Virginia.

Mary Haney has taught for twenty-three years with the Memphis City Schools System. She has taught grades 2 through 7 and has taught elementary computer for five years. For the past seven years, she has been teaching seventh-grade science at Ida B. Wells Academy. Ms. Haney uses technology daily with her seventh-grade science classes. She obtained both her bachelor's and master's degrees in education at the University of Memphis.

Laurence Peters currently directs the Mid-Atlantic Regional Technology in Education Consortium, located at Temple University. Dr. Peters is the author of many articles in the area of technology policy and is currently completing a book (in press) on the global digital divide. He served as senior policy advisor for the U.S. Department of Education and deputy director of the Empowerment Zone and the Enterprise Community Program, where he worked on an initiative to ensure that all Empowerment Zone and Enterprise Community Schools were connected to the Internet. He served as counsel to the Select Education Subcommittee for the House of Representatives for six years and helped author legislation related to authorizing an Office of Educational Technology at the U.S. Department of Education. He holds a Ph.D. from the University of Michigan, Ann Arbor, and a J.D. from the University of Maryland.

Thomas E. Pfundstein currently teaches social studies at Beachwood High School. Prior to that, he spent three years as a seventh-grade social studies teacher at Beachwood Middle School, one year at West Geauga High School, and one year at Cleveland Central Catholic High School. He is also the author of AOL@SCHOOL's weekly online newsletter and a member of the AOL@SCHOOL's Educational Review Panel. He is a doctoral student at the University of Akron in the Curriculum and Instruction Department. His concentration is secondary education (social studies), with an emphasis on Web-based instruction and its impact on teaching and learning. Tom teaches educational technology courses at the University of Akron.

Diane S. Reed is an educational technology consultant and formally an instructional technology specialist for the Fairfax County Public Schools in Virginia. She was the project manager for the K^{12}nects project. Diane has participated in numerous national, state, and local meetings on educational technology. She served as the technology teacher in residence in the Office of Educational Technology at the U. S. Department of Education from 1999 to 2001. Diane is a doctoral candidate at the University of Virginia and is writing her dissertation, "Systemic Technology Infusion: Effects on Teachers and Students."

Christine Richards is the county technology coordinator for the Doddridge County Schools in West Union, West Virginia. As the county's technology coordinator, she works with parents, teachers, business leaders, and concerned citizens to identify technology needs and develop technology plans for the county school system. She troubleshoots technology hardware and software issues in county schools; contacts vendors and prepares bids for technology needs; provides technology and Internet-related training to teachers and parents; searches for technology and Internet resources to improve the quality of education; serves as the county contact for state Internet, SUCCESS, Basic Skills, e-rate, distance learning, online learning, and all other technology initiatives; writes grants; designs and maintains school networks, including wiring; and evaluates hardware and software needs.

Arthur D. Sheekey is the director of the Appalachian Technology in Education Consortium, located at The CNA Corporation in Alexandria, Virginia. Previously, he served as the coordinator for learning technologies for the Council of Chief State School Officers. He is the author of *Education and Telecommunications: Critical Issues and Resources*. Dr. Sheekey was a senior policy analyst in the Office of Educational Research and Improvement at the U.S. Department of Education. He also held positions at the Office of Management and Budget, Office of Plans and Policy at the Federal Communications Commission, and in the White House Office of Science and Technology Policy. He taught high school and junior high school science for five years in New Jersey. He has a B.S. in science from New Jersey City University, an M.A. from Seton Hall University, and a Ph.D. in educational technology from The Catholic University in Washington, D.C.

Robert H. Tai is a former high school physics teacher and curriculum specialist. He developed and implemented a technology-focused curriculum in his Hirschi High School physics class in Wichita Falls, Texas. After earning a Ph.D. at the Harvard University Graduate School of Education, he taught at the City University of New York for three years. He is currently an assistant professor of science education at the Curry School of Education, University of Virginia.

Blake C. West has been a teacher for over twenty years, most spent teaching mathematics and computer science at the high school level in Blue Valley Schools in Overland Park, Kansas. Since 1983, he has provided technology staff development and, in 1998, he became a coordinating teacher for technology in Blue Valley, a position that involves exploring new technologies, advising curriculum committees, team teaching and planning, and creating and providing professional development courses, both face-to-face and online. His support for school improvement and the profession of teaching has been a focus of his work both in Blue Valley and through the NEA. Along the way in his career, he earned a Ph.D. in the first "Instructional Leadership" cadre at the University of Kansas.

Elaine B. Wilkins has taught for twenty years with the Memphis City Schools System and two years with the Memphis Catholic School System. She has taught grades 1 through 8 and has been technology coordinator at Ida B. Wells Academy (a Memphis City School) for seven years. During the 2001–2002 school year, Mrs. Wilkins was technology coach at Ida B. Wells Academy as a part of the Technology Literacy Challenge Fund 2001 grant. She obtained both her bachelor's and master's degrees in education at the University of Memphis.

Eleanor Vernon Wilson has been on the faculty of the Curry School of Education at the University of Virginia since 1991. She is a former elementary school teacher. Her primary teaching responsibilities are in elementary preservice education, and she has collaborated with a Charlottesville, Virginia, elementary school for the past five years to establish a professional development school. Her research interests currently focus on the ways preservice teachers transfer technology skills mastered in the university classroom to varied field placements.